General Editor:
Patrick McNeill

CW00554610

Official Statistics

Martin Slattery

OFFICIAL
STATISTICS

Tavistock Publications · London · New York

First published in 1986 by
Tavistock Publications Ltd
11 New Fetter Lane,
London EC4P 4EE

© 1986 Martin Slattery

Typeset by Hope Services,
Abingdon, Oxfordshire
Printed in Great Britain by
Richard Clay, The Chaucer Press
Bungay, Suffolk

*British Library Cataloguing in
Publication Data*

Slattery, Martin
Official statistics – (Society now) –
(Social science paperbacks; no 337)
1. Statistical services
I. Title   II. Series   III. Series
001.4'22   HA36

ISBN 0–422–60250–7

Contents

Preface

Official statistics are a vital and very rich source of information for anyone interested in seriously analyzing modern society. However the official volumes that contain such facts and figures are often both extremely complex and tedious to read. Chart after chart of innumerable statistics do tend to make most people's heads swim and the official explanations and footnotes only add to the headache.

What this short book attempts to do is to provide an introductory guide through such forests of figures such that even the most innumerate of students (them what can't add up) can follow what they mean and so, I hope, encourage the reader to explore further on his/her own. It also attempts to reveal how such statistics are collected, what they really mean and how they contribute to our store of social knowledge. It's quite a long journey but I have tried to pick the most interesting sights and the most dramatic scenery as a means to aiding understanding and even enjoyment of what, despite first appearances, is a fascinating and relatively unexplored part of our social world.

In this venture I have been aided and abetted, encouraged and bullied, by both Caroline Lane at Tavistock Publications and Pat McNeill, the general editor. Pat's guidance has helped me avoid many a pitfall or accident (though unfortunately he has not been so lucky himself) and I am very grateful for his support and encouragement. Especial thanks too go to Cilla, Ben, Rachel, and Henry who have tolerated and supported Dad's absences into the wilderness of scribbling, and to May Morris for her patience and professionalism in typing this manuscript.

Martin Slattery

PART I
Introducing official statistics

1

Introduction

'There are three kinds of lies: lies, damned lies,
and statistics.' (Benjamin Disraeli)

'Get the facts first and then you can distort
them as much as you please.' (Mark Twain)

How often have you seen a politician perform like a magician, pulling facts and figures out of a hat and making two and two seem like five? How often have you felt battered and bruised after a classroom debate or a bar room argument in which some smart alec pulls a few statistics out of the air and so leaves you and your opinions sprawled on the floor? How often have you felt that if all the statisticians in the world were laid end to end it would be a good thing? How many of you would agree with the quotations above?

Certainly the popular opinion is that statistics are bemusing and even a little scary. Many people fear them and this fear goes back to schooldays when they suffered for hours on end under statistics' Big Brother – mathematics. Some people even develop 'mathophobia', a sort of number blindness. Their legs turn to jelly and their eyes water whenever a chart full of numbers appears before them. Some students have even gone so far as to rename their statistics course – *sadistics*. Thus for

3

most people statistics seem like a jungle, a swamp, or a minefield they fear venturing into in case they get swallowed up by a tribe of calculations or a band of angry equations.

However there are others for whom statistics are God's gift to the truth and the calculator. They keep facts and figures at their fingertips. They are devoted to such numbers and collect them by the bookful. They are statistical disciples. For them social statistics are the untarnished truth and official statistics truly pearls of wisdom – the hardest of hard data, indisputable facts, untainted by human hands, totally reliable, valid, and impartial. And the high priests of this religion (the unsung heroes who dig up these nuggets of knowledge, the magicians who compile the great spells contained in the official tomes that pour forth daily) are the officials of the Government Statistical Service. These are the social archeologists who have ferreted beneath the surface of British society, who have explored deepest Liverpool and chilly Scotland, who have sifted and sorted, cleaned and analyzed the great volumes of *Social Trends* and the *Annual Abstracts*. Official statistics are the very lifeblood of modern bureaucracy, the very food of official thought and the diet of official planning, without which they would starve to death and wither away in a cloud of red tape. Without the facts officials cannot advise, ministers plan, or governments act.

Thus social statistics are more than just facts and figures; they are a source of power. Whoever possesses such knowledge can control governments and mystify the masses, bemuse their neighbours and spellbind an audience. Who could possibly challenge the authority of an official statistic? Well, I hope that by the end of this book you can! The aim of this book is to try to dispel such illusions and to teach you how to handle statistics, how to criticize them, and, most important, to understand how they were made, by whom, and in whose image. Despite their appearance of immutable truth, social statistics – even official ones – are human *creations*. They are not like shells on a seashore or gold in a gold mine – things waiting to be discovered – but are a particular form of human knowledge cast in a mathematical mould. Similarly despite appearances they are far from the driest of dry subjects, only of interest to those with a head for figures. Rather they are a mine of information indispensable to anyone with a serious interest in the shape, structure, and future of modern society. No budding sociologist can do without them and even the most inept of mathematicians (even those who thought two plus two was five) should be able to follow the argument.

The aim of this book therefore is to try to help you understand social statistics, official ones in particular, not as a mathematician but as a sociologist. There are no complicated equations and only one or two 'take-aways'. All you need is an open and inquiring mind, a willingness to learn, and a determination not to be beaten by mere numbers. Essentially this book is a sociological guide through official statistics. It attempts:

- to guide you through the labyrinths of government statistics;
- to direct you toward official and unofficial sources of facts and figures;
- to teach you the skills of interpretation and critical analysis;
- to help you understand the true nature of social statistics – to understand that even these most authoritative of facts and figures are only one form of social knowledge as open to criticism and alternative interpretation as any other. Far from being the end of the search for truth, official statistics are only the beginning. Moreover despite their image, even official statistics do not speak for themselves but are spoken for by that most powerful of bodies, the government, as it attempts to organize, plan, and even control the society it runs.

Introductory guidelines

Before venturing out into the forests of facts and figures it is important to lay down some basic guidelines and issue a few

5

preliminary warnings – a sort of beginner's 'toolkit' to make sure you start out properly equipped. The first important lesson is to make sure you understand exactly what a social statistic is. According to the *Pocket Oxford Dictionary* statistics are 'numerical facts systematically collected on a subject' where facts are taken to be 'things known to be true'. And why do officials go round collecting volumes of social statistics? Well, according to the first volume of *Social Trends* (Government Statistical Service 1970) the aim is to present a manageable selection of statistical material relating to social policies which provides a picture of some significant ways in which our society is changing. Social statistics therefore are no more than social information put into a numerical form. The aim of sound statistical analysis is simply to find out exactly what such numbers really mean, and to do that you need to bear in mind the following points.

How social statistics are defined

The key to sound statistics is clear definition. Without clear definition measurement of a social issue or problem is impossible. Try, for example, defining such basic terms as adult or child. Where does adulthood start – at 16, 18, or 21? – and where does childhood end – 10, 12, 16? Each of these definitions would give you an adult or child population of a different size.

How social statistics are measured

This is the second stage of collecting statistics and the one our maths teacher warned us about – the importance of being accurate, of eliminating errors. Here it is vital to remember that social statistics are essentially *generalizations*. They attempt to represent in numerical form the average or the typical, the general trend, the rate of increase. A wide variety of statistical terms is available, most of which you should be familiar with already – the *ratio*, *rate*, and *percentage*, various forms of *average* (the *mean*, *mode*, and *median*), and the *trend*. Each of these numerical shorthands is extremely useful, but each contains serious dangers. The percentage, for example, is a very useful way of simply indicating increases or decreases, but a good example, too, of the way statistics can be abused. Percentages make sense with large base numbers but can exaggerate small ones. For example, a 20 per cent increase in sexual offences in the City of London in 1983 would sound enough to scare the pants off everyone in the area until you realized that the *total* figure for that year was only fifty-two such crimes and so one 'flasher' on his own could have created this particular 'crime wave'.

Presentation

Rows and rows of figures are often totally meaningless to all but the initiated so they are often presented as charts, graphs, or diagrams to make 'reading' easier. All too often, however, a bar or pie chart can be used to mislead the viewer. Look carefully at the two graphs in *Figure 1.1*. They are in fact exactly the same but have been made to look very different.

Sampling

Apart from a massive social survey every ten years called the census, even most official surveys are based on samples of the population. Sampling, if scientifically conducted, can produce almost as accurate results as a full-scale survey, but if the sample is poorly selected the results will be seriously unrepresentative and biased. You can imagine for example the inaccurate and invalid answers you would get for a survey on family life conducted solely by visiting all the pubs in a particular area. There would be more than a slight bias to the male point of view. The following passage outlines the sampling methods used by one particular sex survey (I told you we would try to make this subject interesting!). What was

Figure 1.1

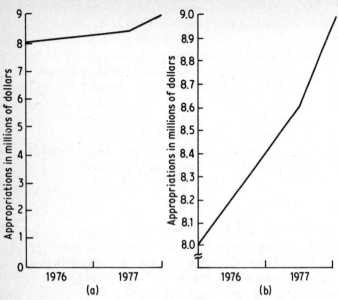

Source: Adapted from Gomm and McNeill (1982).

wrong with this form of sampling? Why would the answers given be unlikely to be a fair representation of the sexual attitudes and behaviour of the 'average' girl today?

'Struth on girls'

Yet another 'revealing' sex survey provided the tabloids last week with eye-swivelling headlines. 'Sexy City Girls on a Five-Night Week' was one example extrapolated from the findings of *Company* magazine, published in the February issue. A sweeping statement, it was gleaned from statistics that appeared to show that 28 per cent of London girls 'enjoy a romp', as a press release put it, five or more times a week – whereas Midlands lasses remain happy on much less sex.

It's when you read on that you discover the investigation was carried out among *Company*'s female readers, 6,000 of whom replied. Most were aged under thirty-five, only a quarter were married or living with someone else. *Company*'s own readership profile is not outlined but, according to a staff member, it is 'an up-market young women's magazine, with well-educated readers who have quite a lot of money to spend'.

This question should also alert you always to check the *response rate* to any survey. All too often exaggerated claims are made by surveys to which only 50 per cent or 40 per cent of people replied, thus ignoring the views of the non-respondents who might well hold very different views. Any survey with a response rate below 70 per cent needs to be treated with caution.

Types of statistic

Be aware too that just as there are all sorts of people so there are different types of statistic. Most statistics are purely 'descriptive': they paint a picture of society by using numbers (population size, crime rate, number of OAPs). Other statistics are more ambitious. They try to identify cause and effect relationships between two or more social variables. However, social statistics do not prove that a causal relationship exists, only that it might. Beware, therefore, the sort of spurious correlation shown by the following example: 'Increased shipments of bananas into the port of Houston have been followed by increases in the national birth rate. Therefore, bananas were the cause of the increase in births' (Sanders 1976).

Social statistics therefore are a form of social measurement and the two main ways of collecting such facts and figures are the social survey and the official register or form. People answer official questionnaires and/or they put their names and details down on official registers, be they at the registry office or the housing department. Such measuring instruments test the social temperature, diagnose the nation's health, or measure society's vital statistics. But like all measuring instruments they are subject to error and the two main forms of error that form the whole basis of this book are those of reliability and validity.

Reliability

This refers both to the accuracy of the measuring instrument and to its consistency; it refers both to the precision and lack of error in an official register or survey and to its ability to produce consistent and reliable results.

However, whilst scientific and technical measuring instruments are generally extremely reliable – highly accurate and dependable – social science ones are not. They are subject to all sorts of errors as they attempt to measure people's vital statistics – their age, occupation, and income – and their opinions. People lie, exaggerate, and simply forget. People are missed out even in that most thorough of official surveys, the census.

Validity

This refers to the extent to which a measuring instrument actually measures what it claims to be measuring. Whilst a watch obviously measures time and a thermometer measures body temperature, does an IQ test really measure intelligence, *No!* or occupation a person's social standing? Such questions are at the forefront of every section of this book. How far do social statistics reflect the attitudes and behaviour of ordinary people and how far do they reflect the attitudes and values of those doing the measuring? How far does the *definition* used by the social researcher predetermine the final results? Try defining such apparently simple social concepts as crime and poverty and you will start to realize how crucial a precise definition is to both the reliability and validity of social statistics. As we shall see later, all too easily official statistics are more a measurement of officials and their attitudes than of the criminals, suicide victims, or strikes they claim to be describing.

Thus whilst reliability refers mainly to 'technical' problems of error and inaccuracy, validity is more concerned with theoretical and conceptual problems, of how a social fact was defined. Validity is more important than reliability. Even if a measurement was 100 per cent reliable it would not be valid if it was measuring the wrong thing. Similarly if the definition changes, so will the measurement. If the official male retirement age in Britain was reduced to sixty, then overnight the population of OAPs would increase dramatically.

These two concepts – reliability and validity – form the crux of this book and will be the basis of most of the analyses that follow. They even form the basis of the main distinctions between the various sociological perspectives, in particular positivism and phenomenology.

Sponsorship and interpretation

Finally in any analysis of social statistics, even such apparently harmless and impersonal ones as official statistics, it is important to ask who collected the facts and figures and why. Why was this particular social issue or problem chosen for investigation and not some other? How were the concepts involved defined, how was the data interpreted, and what will the results be used for? Such questions are essentially *political* ones – not in the party political sense (though obviously statistics are an important part of the political party propaganda battle) but in the broader sense that all forms of social knowledge represent *power*: the power to inform or mislead, the power to illuminate or manipulate. Whoever controls the definition of official statistics controls what is collected and how much; whoever controls the interpretation of official statistics controls public debate (and criticism); whoever has the power to withhold official data (or not collect it in the first place) has the power to prevent public discussion from arising.

Thus despite their appearance of political neutrality and impartiality even official statistics are a key source of political power, and though it is often claimed that such facts and figures are incontrovertible and can speak for themselves, they do have to be interpreted. As we shall see they are open to alternative interpretations; they are occasionally used to defend, even to 'whitewash', government actions and policies. As Jack Brand (1975) has somewhat cynically pointed out, for governments:

> 'The procedure is simple and well known. When you are threatened by some unpleasant development, do a statistical appraisal of the situation. Unless you are extremely unlucky you will be able to get some figures which will justify you in doing what you were going to do anyway – often nothing.'

Thus it is vital to bear in mind that the collection and analysis of even official statistics is not simply a 'technical' process but a highly ideological and political one involving a series of social actors, as the chart opposite illustrates (*Figure 1.2*).

1. The investigator – e.g. the General Register Office which carries out the population census.
2. The client – e.g. a government department or a local government authority.
3. The collector of the information – e.g. the registrar who receives notifications of births, marriages, and deaths.
4. The respondent or informant who supplies the information – e.g. the head of the household; the father who notifies a birth; the national government.
5. The independent user or the critic or anyone besides the client who uses the information – e.g. the public who are informed by the news media; the media themselves who are informed by referring to the investigators' reports; an academic researcher.

Figure 1.2

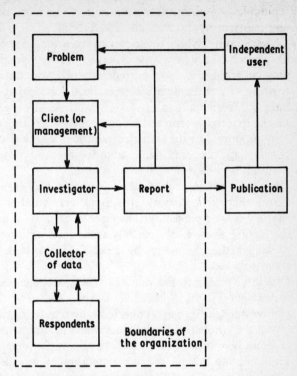

Source: OU D291G *Statistical Sources*.

Guidelines to statistical analysis – a summary

Below is a checklist of the key points to look for whenever you are faced with a set of statistics, be they official or unofficial. Bear these points in mind and you should avoid the worst of the pitfalls before you. Some of the points below we have covered already, while others will become clearer as this book progresses.

1. Check the source of the statistics involved. The more reputable and authoritative the source the more reliable and trustworthy the data and conclusions.
2. Check who sponsored the survey or statistics. Look for the likelihood that these statistics have been manipulated or only collected to support a predetermined case. Check the reasons why the statistics were collected and what use is intended for them.
3. Check that the interpretations and conclusions reached are fully supported by the statistics published. Check that such conclusions are reasonable and logical and not mere opinion or conjecture.
4. Check the statistics themselves for error and distortion. Check that the statistical terms used were valid and fair, that a rate or a percentage hasn't been used to exaggerate the picture given. Look carefully at the chart or graph used to see whether the figures have been made to look better than they are.
5. Check the reliability and validity of the collecting/measuring instrument:
- † How were the statistics collected – by register or survey?
- † Was the whole population questioned or only a *sample*? If a sample was used check such factors as the sample size, the sampling frame, the way the sample was selected (random, quota, etc.), the response rate, etc.
- † How was the questionnaire designed? How were its concepts defined, its questions worded? Were there any ambiguities or complications?
6. Check for missing data. Why was some information missed out? Might it have altered the results/conclusions?

N.B. Never accept any statistics on face value. They are like people; they often change once you get to know them better.

The layout of this book

This book is divided into three main sections:
  Chapter 2 is a detailed description of official statistics:

14

- their background;
- their sources and types, in particular the 1981 census.

Chapters 3 to 8 attempt to go deeper into official statistics, attempt to help you develop both the technical skills and the sociological awareness necessary for understanding, analyzing, and criticizing such authoritative facts and figures by taking you through a series of case studies. Each chapter topic is designed not only to tackle a key area of social life but to illustrate a particular skill and make you think like a sociologist. Various examples and activities are set throughout to get you to develop and practice your critical and analytical faculties, and to get you to appreciate and question the official picture of Britain.

Chapter 9 brings you up for air and tries to give some understanding of the way social statistics are produced. You are asked to look closer at the 'mechanics' of statistical collection and at the influences upon this process which can drastically alter the *meaning* of the statistics produced.

With a few exceptions all the statistics used refer to British society and the appendices direct you towards sources of both official and 'alternative' statistics.

Thus I hope you will emerge from this assault course in the sociology of statistics with the skills and perceptions necessary for handling official statistics with confidence in the future and, even more important, a thirst for more. Your appetite should have been whetted and your teeth sharpened for next year's *Social Trends* or next month's unemployment figures. So if you enjoy a good argument, if you relish the devastating insight, the cool analysis, or the alternative interpretation, if you will only respect the detailed answer, the accurate figure, and hate the exaggeration or the unsubstantiated claim, then this is the book for you. Happy hunting!

Activities

1. The annual incomes of twenty-five employees of a firm are:

1 receives £25 000 (managing director)
1 receives £7600
2 receive £5500
1 receives £3800
3 receive £3500
4 receive £2500
1 receives £2100
12 receive £1400

Calculate the mean annual income ... (£3472)
Calculate the median annual income ... (£2100)
Calculate the modal annual income ... (£1400)

Which figures will you quote if you are the managing director, and which if you are the union representative, in a press release concerning a recent pay claim?
Source: Gomm and McNeill (1982).

2. True or false?
(a) Children of unskilled manual workers are killed on the roads at a higher rate than the children of professional workers. This shows that they are less well cared for.
(b) There is a higher suicide rate in Denmark than in Britain. This shows that the permissive society leads to unhappiness.
(c) More people are murdered by a close relative or friend than by a stranger. It is therefore safer to go for a walk with a stranger than with your father.
(d) 97.2 per cent of boys who entered for 'A' level Greek in England and Wales in 1977 passed the examination. 38.3 per cent who entered for domestic science passed. Greek is therefore much easier than domestic science.
Source: Gomm and McNeill (1982).

Further reading

There are a whole variety of introductory statistics books.

The following are readable, amusing, and highlight the pitfalls of statistical analysis:

Hastings (1979)
Hooke (1983)
Huff (1973)
Reichmann (1964)
Sanders (1976)

2

Official statistics

Introduction

Having laid down some basic guidelines we now come to the meat of this book – *official statistics*: what they say, what they mean, and why they are collected. After looking briefly at the history of official statistics, we look in detail at the main sources of official facts and figures and the picture they paint of British society today.

The history of official statistics

Though the census and official departments of statistics are very recent phenomena, the collection of facts and figures by government about its people is as old as the most ancient of civilizations, beyond William the Conqueror's *Domesday Book*, beyond even Herod's survey at the time of the birth of Christ. However such population 'counts' were very limited.

They had only two main purposes – the collection of taxes and the conscription of able-bodied men into the king's army. The word statistics itself derives from the Latin *status* or political state and the German *statistik* or *state-istic*, facts and figures for the use of the state. Such 'political' arithmetic however did not become either properly organized or scientific until the scientific revolution in Europe in the seventeenth century and the growth of European nationalism. Every nation state was now determined to gather as many facts as possible about their populations, trade, finance, taxes, and armed forces in the fierce balance of power between such states as Bismark's Germany and Napoleon III's France.

However even by the early twentieth century the official collection and analysis of social statistics was very limited and amateurish. It took two world wars, the pioneering efforts of social surveyors like Charles Booth and Seebohm Rowntree, and the post-war demand by the electorate for the government to provide both economic management and a welfare state to put British official statistics on a professional footing. The Government Statistical Service (GSS) was set up in 1941 and expanded thereafter from population statistics to those on economic, social, and psychological issues. Under the leadership of Claus Moser and the patronage of Harold Wilson the GSS became an integral part of the 1960s Labour government's attempt to modernize Britain. It grew to over 500 professional staff and over 6,000 support staff and established an international reputation for its sheer professionalism. However amid the depression of the 1970s and the 'cuts' of the 1980s, the GSS has had both its size and status pruned.

Sources of official statistics

Nevertheless in serving modern government the GSS and its agencies produce such a wealth of facts and figures every year that an 'official guide' has to be published for even academic experts to find their way round the volumes produced. The GSS however is not a giant 'fact-finding factory' as in Canada or the EEC but a relatively decentralized organization made up of the statistics divisions of all the major government departments plus the two main collecting agencies – the Business Statistics Office and the Office of Population Censuses and Surveys (OPCS) – with the Central Statistical Office (CSO) co-ordinating the whole system. The major collection of official statistics is the census – the subject of the next section. More regular and up-to-date official statistics are collected by:

1. The registration and administrative procedures of a variety of government departments like the Registrar General.
2. Official sample surveys, the most important of which are *multipurpose surveys*. Whilst national statistics offer a static picture of British society, a sort of snapshot, multipurpose surveys offer a continuous picture revealing the general trends and dynamics of social change. The three most important for our purposes are the following.

THREE MOST IMP. ARE?

The Family Expenditure Survey (FES)

This is a fortnightly diary completed by a random sample of 11,000 households outlining their weekly and monthly expenditure patterns. It includes questions on income and such outgoings as food, clothing, drink, heat and light, insurances and credit payments. It began in the 1950s and is a unique source of highly reliable information on household income and expenditure. It is however limited by its response rate (70 per cent) and by referring only to households not individuals or families.

The General Household Survey (GHS)

This was started in 1971 by the OPCS as a means to covering gaps in other sources of official statistics, gaps in time, in detail, in testing relationships between social variables and between official surveys. It is not tied to any one single topic and so is very flexible and can be easily adapted to new social trends or official needs. It covers five main subject areas – population, housing, employment, education, and health – and it is based on a stratified sample of 15,000 households selected from the electoral register. It is very reliable and has an exceptional response rate (84 per cent).

The Labour Force Survey (LFS)

This began in 1973 when Britain joined the Common Market. It is a survey on the size and structure of the labour force carried out every two years in collaboration with the member countries of the EEC to aid Community policy-making on such issues as regional development and to provide a basis for distributing the social fund to 'needy' areas. It offers invaluable information on the whole European picture and provides an important basis for comparing and improving British statistics.

A list of the other major official surveys is given below and backed up by about 250 'ad hoc' government surveys; it shows the enormous sweep and depth of detail available to both officials and sociologists, covering everything apparently possible from national readership to working conditions, ethnic groups to contraception.

All this information is regularly published as follows.

General digests

1. The *Monthly Digest of Statistics* – a monthly collection and update of all official statistics ranging from population through to finance and the weather.
2. The *Annual Abstract of Statistics* – probably the most authoritative and most quoted of official publications. It dates back to the mid-nineteenth century and covers just about every aspect of economic, social, and industrial life.

Table 2.1 Some other major surveys

	frequency	date	sampling frame	sample size	unit of analysis	type of respondent	response rate (%)	location
National Food Survey	continuous from	1940	electoral register	15,000	households	housewife	52	GB
International Passenger Survey	continuous from	1964	international passengers at ports, airports, etc.	260,000	individual traveller	individual traveller	88	GB
New Earnings Survey	annual from	1970	national insurance numbers	170,000	employees	employers	82	GB
Survey of Personal Incomes	annual from	1954/5	inland revenue records	144,000	tax units	local tax offices	95	UK
English House Condition Survey	irregular from	1967	valuation list	9,000	households	household heads	83	E
National Dwelling and Housing Survey	ad hoc	1977/9	valuation list	915,000	households and individuals	one adult in household	85	GB
National Readership Survey	continuous from	1956	electoral register	30,000	individuals	individuals	75	GB
EEC Consumer Attitude Survey	four-monthly from	1974	electoral register	12,000	individuals	household heads	84	GB
National Child Development Survey	ad hoc surveys of cohort	1958	birth records	17,000	individuals in cohort	cohort members and others	87	GB
National Training Survey	ad hoc	1975/6	electoral register	54,000	individuals	working adults	72	GB
Workplace Industrial Relations Survey	three-yearly from	1980	census of employment	2,700	establishments	managers and worker representatives	76	GB
National Travel Survey	regular from	1965	electoral register	15,000	individuals	households heads	85	GB

Its tables cover time-spans of ten years or more, thus highlighting trends and allowing comparison.

3. *Social Trends* – probably the most 'popular' of official publications. It is colourfully illustrated, easy to read, and covers all the main sociological areas as well as providing occasional essays on particular topics: 'The government's bumper annual fact-pack on the state of Britain' was how *The Times* referred to it.

4. *Regional Trends* – similarly readable and illustrated, this publication provides a regional breakdown of the national statistics in *Social Trends*.

5. *Economic Trends* – an 'economic' version of *Social Trends* covering the main economic indicators, statistics and trends in the UK economy. For more detailed economic analysis there is also:

(a) *British Business* – a collection of statistics and commentary from the Department of Trade and Industry;

(b) The *UK National Accounts* (the CSO *Blue Book*) and the *UK Balance of Payments* (the CSO *Pink Book*) – sort of national and international balance sheets covering ten years or more;

(c) The *Economic Progress Report* – a monthly publication by the Treasury providing official analysis and background on government policy and on the current economic situation.

Scotland, Wales and N. Ireland have similar publications of their own.

Departmental publications

Each government department also collects and publishes its own statistics (see Appendix A for a list of useful addresses). Examples include the *Defence Statistics* and the Department of the Environment's statistics on the homeless. For our purposes though three publications are especially useful:

1. *Population Trends* – a quarterly publication of tables and articles by the OPCS on a wide range of demographical and medical issues. It also produces useful series and fact packs for schools.
2. *Criminal Statistics, England and Wales* – produced by the Home Office (Scotland has a separate legal system and set of statistics) and covering an enormous range of criminal activities from gambling to terrorism, as well as the general trends in crime, sentencing, and police prosecution.
3. The *Employment Gazette* – published monthly by the Department of Employment, it provides up-to-date statistics on all forms of employment, unemployment, and economic activity, plus very useful articles on how such statistics are defined and collected.

There is also *Britain – An Official Handbook*, the CSO update magazine *Statistical News*, and most especially for a student's purposes the CSO's little pocket reference card 'The UK in figures' which summarizes the main official facts and figures.

Behind all these official surveys and publications, though, lies the 'Big Daddy' of them all, the *census*.

The census

This is the most authoritative, comprehensive and detailed national survey there is. It is so large, so expensive, and so thorough that even the government can only afford to conduct one every ten years and it takes at least five years fully to digest and analyse. As David Rhind explains:

> 'The Census of Population is certainly a major decennial event in Britain: the taking of the 1981 Census involved the employment of more than 129,000 people, cost about £45 million and was designed to elicit information from every one of the twenty million or so households in this country.'
> (Rhind 1983)

24

This enormous official undertaking takes years of planning (plans for 1991 are already underway) and as David Rhind (1983) points out, it 'is the most important single source of information about the number and condition of the people' because it is so thorough, detailed, and regular.

Censuses in one form or another can be dated back to the Ancient Egyptians, Greeks, and Romans but modern censuses – in the sense of being detailed and regular – have only occurred in Europe since the nineteenth century.

The first full British census was carried out in 1801 and every ten years thereafter. But it wasn't until 1841 that detailed information was asked and the 'head of household' made the main respondent. This followed the Civil Registration Act of 1837, the establishment of the office of Registrar General under the commissionship of Dr William Farr. From then on all vital statistics – of births, deaths, marriages, etc. – had to be registered in England and Wales (but not until 1855 in Scotland). The legal basis for the census was established by the 1920 Census Act which made completion of the census form compulsory and allowed Parliament to authorize each census simply by an Order in Council.

The 1981 census

This was the eighteenth in Great Britain. It was taken on 5 April, 1981. It had the shortest census form in the last fifty years, asking only twenty-one questions as in the chart in *Figure 2.1.*

It covered 54,128,000 people and generated over 2,500 million items of information. According to the present Registrar General for England and Wales, A.R. Thatcher, it cost about £45 million at 1980 prices, about £1 per head of population. After debates in Parliament one question – on ethnicity – was excluded, but otherwise the whole operation went off virtually without incident.

'Incredibly, the main concerns at the time in England and Wales were the number of enumerators who were bitten by

Figure 2.1 The 21 questions in the 1981 census

Population items

1 Name

2 Sex

3 Date of birth

4 Marital status (single, married, remarried, divorced, widowed)

5 Relationship in household (husband/wife/son/daughter, other: specified)

6 Whereabouts on census night

7 Usual address (including postcode)

8 Usual address: 1 year ago (including postcode)

9 Country of birth (present name of country)

10 Whether working, retired, housewife, etc., last week (full-time, part-time)

11 Name and business of employer

12 Occupation (includes description of work)

13 Employment status (apprentice, supervisory role, self-employed)

14 Address of place of work (including postcode)

15 Daily journey to work (train, tube, bus, van, foot etc.)

16 Degrees, professional and vocational qualifications

Housing items

H1 Number of rooms

H2 Tenure (freehold, leasehold, renting, other)

H3 Amenities (fixed bath or shower connected, WC)

H4 Shared household

H5 Cars and vans (number)

Source: Population Trends 36, summer 1984.

guard dogs, and problems of access to certain areas where there was foot and mouth disease. Although there were (as always) some critics of the Census form, the great majority of people completed it without any difficulty.'

(Thatcher 1984)

For census purposes England and Wales is divided into just over 100,000 enumeration districts, each containing on average 180 households. An enumerator is appointed to each district to deliver and collect the forms and advise people on how to complete them. People are counted by the census in their home (or someone else's home) at a fixed time. In the 1981 census this was at midnight on Sunday, 5 April. The census form refers to a household defined as: 'A household comprises either one person living alone or a group of persons (who may or may not be related) living at the same address with common housekeeping.'

The census form (see Appendix B) asked for information about each member of the household and anyone else present at that time. But it also sought information about the household as a unit and every British census has been essentially one of population and housing. People in other institutions (schools, hospitals, hotels etc.) were asked the same information. Out of nearly 18 million households in 1981 less than 6,000 failed or refused to complete the census form and only 700 people were actually prosecuted for such dereliction of duty.

Although each individual question produced a lot of information, so too did cross-analyses of questions. For example cross-referencing questions on sex, marital status, and relationship in the household provides a detailed analysis of the structure of the modern British family, whilst that on age is used by officials for determining grants to local authorities, for making national and local population projections, and for estimating the future income and expenditure of the social security system. Note here that the census form asks date of birth rather than age as generally people are more accurate about this information than remembering how old they are. Similarly the census is the only source of comprehensive information on migrants (both within Britain and from overseas) and of the 'working' population. Question eight (usual address one year ago) may seem pretty innocuous but in fact it is used to tap population movements out of the inner city, around the country, and abroad; whilst questions ten to fifteen fill in important gaps in Department of Employment information on the 'unregistered' unemployed – the self-employed and apprentices.

Comments and criticisms

Inevitably in such a massive operation errors occur. Some people are missed entirely, some double-counted; some characteristics such as age and occupation are wrongly recorded, wrongly coded or wrongly key-punched. In the processing of the 1981 census there were 100,000 keying errors according to the Registrar General's Review. Certain social groups seem especially vulnerable to 'getting lost' – the old, adolescents, and infants (as all their ages are likely to get distorted), and immigrants. Such omissions may well affect the overall picture of these particular groups.

Second, many of the definitions (though pre-tested) may lead to misinformation due to ambiguity or misunderstanding. Question H1 on the number of rooms has led to a lot of problems in every census (think about it!) and question twelve on occupation is especially prone to people exaggerating their actual job.

Third, the British census is much more limited than most other countries' and does not include questions on such topics as religion, income, and race. This may reflect British respect for personal privacy but from a sociological point of view it does mean valuable social information is missed out.

Extensive checks are made by the OPCS to eliminate errors and gaps – for example they undertake a re-run of the census shortly after census day and extensive cross-checks are made with other sources of data like the GHS. The OPCS estimates however that the 1981 population count was only half a per cent below the true figure (only 240,000 people were missed out of 54 million or more), a classic example of the professionalism and reliability of British census data.

The advantages and disadvantages of official statistics

Obviously the main advantage of using official social statistics is simply the great wealth of information available on a very wide range of economic, social, and political issues. Such data is readily available and often the only information produced on many topics. Official statistics allow the examination of trends over time, comparisons between social groups and geographical regions, and 'before and after studies', enabling sociologists to examine the effects for example of legislation like the 1972 Raising of the School Leaving Age or 1971 Divorce Reform Act.

However official statistics do also have their limitations and problems from a sociological point of view:

- They are collected essentially for official, administrative, and political purposes. Often therefore they do not cover areas of particular interest to sociologists (or only in passing) such as income and wealth.
- Official definitions are often non-sociological and would be seriously criticized by sociologists as we shall see later.
- Comparisons between censuses and even official surveys like the GHS are often very difficult because definitions have been changed or no longer 'mean' the same. Moreover due to the time taken to plan and publish official surveys their definitions tend to be out of date in a world that is changing so rapidly.
- Much official data is not published or is inaccessible either because of the cost involved or for political reasons. To avoid embarrassment governments occasionally withhold information or limit its publication (e.g. the *Black Report on Health in Britain* – see Townsend and Davidson 1980 – was originally published as a mere 260 duplicated copies by the DHSS).

Finally official statistics only provide 'quantitative' data. There are no official statistics on British public opinion or attitudes – though the establishment of the *British Social Attitudes Survey* described below is a step in that direction.

Social attitudes

The statistics above have all been purely factual and objective ones. Officials carefully avoid collecting statistics on attitudes and beliefs due to the inherent difficulties of subjective data. It is less reliable and much more difficult to define. However in 1983–4 the Departments of Employment and the Environment did help sponsor a national survey of British social attitudes by sociologists at Social and Community Planning Research. Moreover its directors, Roger Jowell and Colin Airey, were given official blessing by being allowed to write a leading article for the 1985 *Social Trends*. This semi-official survey was designed to cover the enormous gap in our social knowledge left by the official statistics, by trying to show what British people think as well as what they do. Such an annual national survey of a sample of 1,761 adults (a 70 per cent response rate) attempts to reveal the British character and culture in the way the *General Social Survey* does in America. The *British Social Attitudes Survey* (Jowell and Airey 1984) showed for example that in terms of political attitudes, though the British electorate is still very volatile and even politically active, it still has a strong underlying faith in such traditional institutions as the monarchy, the BBC, and the police. However there is a general public scepticism about the ability of the government to solve our economic crisis and a widespread fear of the social effects of unemployment. Whilst many people favour private health and education there is a general desire for a strong and comprehensive health service and a growing recognition of the extent of poverty in Britain today. On issues of a social or moral nature the survey revealed widespread prejudice in terms of race, class, and sex, with around a third of the total sample describing themselves as prejudiced against people of other races.

The problems of attitude surveys

Such attitudinal surveys have even greater problems of

reliability and validity than factual ones, as Jowell and Airey (1984) themselves point out:

- First, there is no such thing as the 'man in the street' nor even a public opinion. Rather there are a whole variety of publics each with their own opinion.
- Second, public attitudes do not divide simply into a single continuum. You cannot simply label people as left or right-wing, conservative or liberal. Rather their attitudes vary according to the issue involved, and whilst age may be the main influence on some opinions, on other topics sex is. Moreover people are often inconsistent, holding conflicting, even contradictory, views in many cases. Jowell and Airey therefore concluded that it is doubtful that there is a 'common British attitudinal culture – waiting to be discovered'.
- Third, there is always the danger in such surveys that the questionnaire is actually *creating* opinions. Because of the very fact that they are being asked for an opinion people often give one, even though they have never thought about the issue before. Moreover the opinions given in an interview situation are not necessarily a true reflection of actual behaviour. It was surprising quite so many people actually admitted to being racially prejudiced in the 1984 survey.
- Fourth, with a survey that has only been going for three years so far it is obviously not yet possible to analyze trends in public opinion, though this is the long-term aim. Nevertheless by using a panel of interviewees (553) the researchers were able to examine shifts in opinion between 1983 and 1984 in more detail, to show for example a growth in desertions from the Conservative Party.
- Fifth, it is similarly very difficult as yet to analyze two or three-way 'cause and effect' relationships, until public opinion(s) settle down more and 'spurious' correlations can be eliminated.

Despite such problems though, the *British Social Attitudes*

Survey is a major project of enormous importance in both assessing public opinion and in supporting official factual statistics. We can now try to analyze not only what the British public does, but why it does it (or at least why it thinks it does it).

Non-official sources of social statistics

Besides the wealth of data produced by the GSS, CSO, and government departments there is also a great deal of semi-official, unofficial, and private statistics available produced by business, local authorities, market research companies, self-help groups, pressure groups, radical organizations, and academic institutions. A full list of these is given in Appendix A. Such sources are invaluable for:

- filling in gaps in official statistics;
- providing alternative statistics that highlight weaknesses in official data and provide the basis for critical analysis.

Conclusions

These then are the main sources of official facts and opinions about Britain today. As they show, a veritable treasure trove of facts and figures is available to the sociologist attempting to study the past, present, and future from both an official and unofficial perspective.

This chapter has painted a broad sweep of official statistics. What we go on to now is a series of detailed case studies of individual sociological topics, each of immense interest in themselves but each also used to illustrate the strengths and weaknesses of official statistics, to demonstrate alternative interpretations, and to provide practice in developing the tools and the skills of the sociological trade – how not to be blinded by statistical science!

Activities

1. Send away for a copy of 'UK in Figures' available free

from CSO Information Services Division, Cabinet Office, Great George Street, London SW1, and draw up your own statistical map of modern Britain.

2. Look at *Table 2.1* again and say which official survey(s) you would look at for information on each of the following:
   (a) The state of housing in England;
   (b) What the British public reads;
   (c) Tourism at home and abroad.

   What sampling frames do the following surveys use and why:

   (a) *NES* (b) *IPS* (c) *GHS* (see *Table 2.1*, p. 22).

   Why would the *Survey of Personal Incomes* be considered a highly reliable source of information but the *National Food Survey* a far less reliable one?

3. Look at the 1981 census questionnaire (Appendix B) and try completing page one of it yourself. Make a list of any questions you found difficult to understand or answer. Make a list of any questions that you would like to have seen included in the census in addition to the list of questions on p. 26.

4. Pick a topic such as poverty, unemployment, or housing. Write away for both official and unofficial information using the list of addresses in Appendix A. Compare the different statistics and interpretations you get back.

Further reading

The best outline of the census is by David Rhind (1983) whilst Catherine Hakim's (1982) study is an authoritative overview of official statistical sources.

   Roger Jowell and Colin Airey's series, British Social

Attitudes Survey, is developing into an annual account of what the British think – and very revealing it is too.

For those statistical masterminds amongst you, try Tony Osman's 'The Facts of Everyday Life' (1985), whilst for those who like having their brains teased, Michael Williams' series for 'New Society' is now available in a book! Britain Now Quiz (1985).

PART II
Case studies in official statistics

3

Population: demographic statistics – an exercise in statistical description

Case studies in official statistics

This chapter and the five following ones examine in detail a wide variety of sociological topics. They outline what the official statistics in each of these areas apparently say and then scrutinize such conclusions from alternative viewpoints as a way of illustrating how even the most official of facts and figures are not self-explanatory – how much statistics are influenced, even created, by social and political influences. We start with population as a basis for illustrating basic statistical data and basic skills and then progress through to such social statistics as class, gender, suicide, and crime, developing from there into such overtly political statistics as unemployment and the distribution of wealth. By taking each analysis a step at a time we hope to gradually build up your understanding not only of what official statistics say but why they are saying it, not only of how to 'read' official statistics but how to understand what they mean in the broadest sense of the word.

Introduction to population statistics

Population statistics are the most basic of official statistics and one of the key reasons censuses were introduced. They represent the hardest of hard data, the most stable, impartial, and value-free of official statistics. After all, what possible alternative interpretation could you put on the size of a country's population? What possible errors could occur apart from missing a few thousand people out? From its early objectives of counting populations as a basis for taxation and raising armies (and tackling health problems) *demography* has become an academic 'science' in its own right and is central to the social and economic planning of modern government.

Demography has been defined as 'the scientific study of human populations with respect to their size, their structure and their development' (*UN Multilingual Demographic Dictionary* 1958). The four key features of a demographic analysis are:

1. The size of the population;
2. The age and sex distribution of the population;
3. Fertility and mortality rates, i.e. birth and death statistics;
4. The movement of the population in and out of the country, i.e. immigration and emigration.

Each of these factors is important in its own right but what is crucial is the *balance* between them, the balance between, for example, the birth and death rates or immigration and emigration. Crucial too is the *structure* of the population – the balance between the sexes or age groups. The central aim of demography is the establishment of *reliable* statistics on such factors as birth and death rates, marriages and divorces, life expectancy, and so on.

Activity

Instead of me describing the main features of Britain's population trends it seemed much more useful for you to do it and so gain practice in reading statistical data. To make it easier and more interesting we have chosen charts produced by *Barclays Bank Review* (1985) which present official statistics in a very dramatic and eye-catching way (note the importance of presentation, p. 7). Use the following questions simply as an initial guide and once you are used to looking at these facts and figures draw up your own analysis.

Questions

(a) What was Britain's population in 1801? What is it today (*Figure 3.1*)?

(b) What are the major factors determining the size of a country's population? Why did Britain have a population explosion in the nineteenth century and baby booms in the twentieth century?

(c) What key trends can be identified in the distribution and movement of population in and between the main regions of the UK? Try to explain such trends (*Figure 3.2*).

(d) Explain the following terms: (i) 'labour force', (ii) 'ageing population', and their importance in social analysis and planning.

(e) How is the changing role of women having a key effect on the demographic size, structure, and the labour force of modern Britain?

(f) *Figure 3.6* shows British population trends and their economic implications. It shows the wide variety of predictions as to Britain's likely future population. Such *trends* are based on 'extrapolating' present demographic trends into the future.

   (i) Why do you think so many of these predictions have been proved wrong (think particularly again about the changing role of women)?

Figure 3.1   Growth of UK population

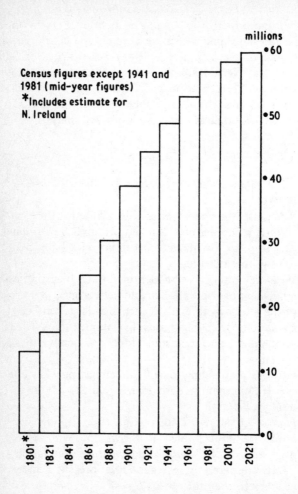

Census figures except 1941 and 1981 (mid-year figures)
*Includes estimate for N. Ireland

millions
•60
•50
•40
•30
•20
•10
•0

1801* 1821 1841 1861 1881 1901 1921 1941 1961 1981 2001 2021

Sources (Figs 3.1–3.4): CSO Annual Abstract of Statistics, Population Projections 1981–2021, OPCS (Crown copyright: reproduced with permission of the Controller of HMSO.)

40

Figure 3.2 Regional population growth
%

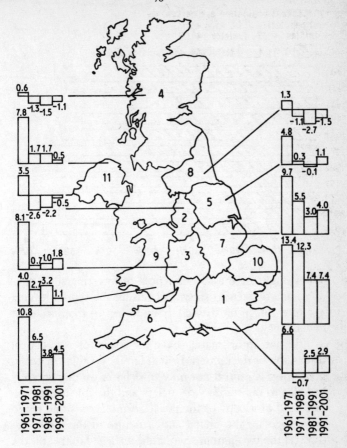

(ii) Why are such predictions so important to government planning and what damage is caused to the
planning of roads, schools, hospitals, etc. when such
extrapolations are proved wrong?

(g) Try defining the terms 'old age pensioner' and 'immi-
grant'.

Figure 3.3 The welfare burden

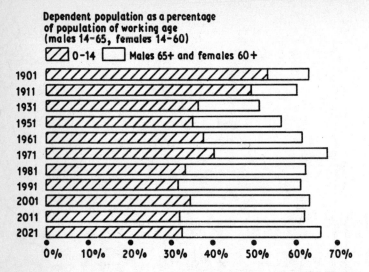

Dependent population as a percentage
of population of working age
(males 14–65, females 14–60)

▨ 0–14   ☐ Males 65+ and females 60+

(h) What might be the consequences of lowering the retirement age of men to sixty and raising the school-leaving age to eighteen on (i) the labour force, (ii) the burden of dependency.

(i) We do not unfortunately have the space for a statistical discussion of the modern British family yet this key social institution is central not only to debates on demography but also to the stability of society and the role of women. Get hold of a copy of the latest *Social Trends* and try to piece together the 'shape and structure of the family today' (is the two-parent, two-child nuclear family still the norm?) and examine the effect of divorce – is it shattering modern family life or stabilizing it?

Further reading

David Hubback's (1983) booklet for the Simon Population Trust, *Population Trends in Great Britain: Their Policy*

Figure 3.4   Age and sex distribution

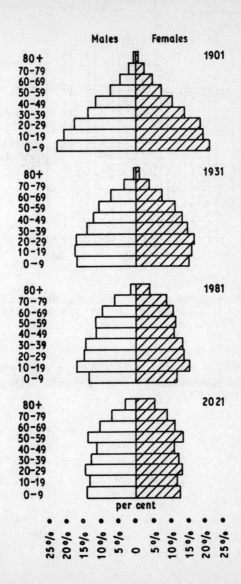

Figure 3.5 The labour force

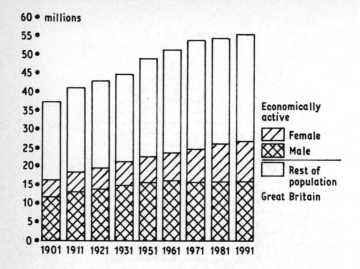

Sources: British Labour Statistics, Historical Abstract 1886–1968, Department of Employment Gazette, February 1984. (Crown copyright: reproduced with permision of the Controller of HMSO.)

Implications, is a useful summary of present demographic trends and summarizes Dr John Ermisch's analysis of its causes. Compare his analysis to your own.

Figure 3.6 Actual and projected population of the United Kingdom

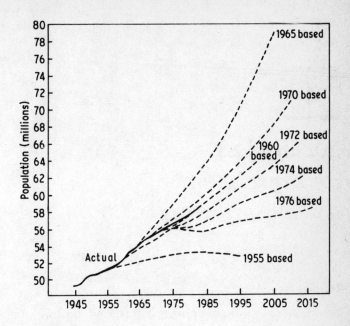

Source: OPCS from Eversley and Köllman (1982). (Crown copyright: reproduced with permission of the Controller of HMSO.)

4

Social class –
an exercise in
social indicators

Introduction

So far our discussion has primarily been concerned with raw
or basic social statistics. However social statistics are often
used to measure or *indicate* the state of society, to represent
some underlying social phenomenon that cannot be measured
directly, so that one or more social statistics must be used as
an 'indirect' measure. For example the Retail Price Index is
used to indicate changes in the cost of living and even to
measure inflation, whilst a battery of statistics such as those
on crime, suicide, divorce, unemployment, etc. are used to
indicate a society's level of 'stability'. Michael Carley (1981)
has defined social indicators as both surrogates (they stand in
the place of something else) and social measures. The problem
is to operationalize them, to decide what social statistics are a
valid indicator of a particular social phenomenon. How for
example would you measure 'alienation' or urban deprivation?

To illustrate the uses and problems of social indicators we concentrate in this chapter on one particular example – social class.

A case study of a social indicator: social class

This topic is an excellent example of both the virtues and vices of social indicators especially as it is undoubtedly *the* key concept in any sociological analysis. Social class not only refers to the system of social ranking characteristics of advanced industrial societies but to the very way of life, the attitudes, values, and life-chances experienced by different groups of people. It refers not only to such *objective* factors as a person's income, power, status, and education, but to subjective feelings and images, to class 'consciousness' – not only to how people act and behave but how they think and feel. Being middle or working class means more than just having a non-manual or manual job. It affects almost everything a person does from how he votes to what sort of neighbours he has.

However social class is also a very difficult concept to define and measure. As George Orwell has put it:

'Whichever way you turn this curse of class difference confronts you like a wall of stone. Or rather it is not so much like a stone wall as the plate glass pane of an aquarium: it is so easy to pretend that it isn't there, and so impossible to get through it.'

(Orwell 1937)

So to operationalize this concept sociologists have used a surrogate to represent it and the one most widely chosen is *occupation*. A person's job not only tells you a lot about his income, education, and status, but about his lifestyle and general attitudes, and although government officials are very reluctant to employ so vague and unscientific a concept as class they too have used occupation as the basis of the Registrar General's social classification. This divides the

British public into five main classes on the basis of levels of skill, with the middle–working class boundary being in the middle of social class III separating non-manual and manual occupations. *Table 4.1* below shows the official statistics on the social class distribution of the British population today.

As *Table 4.1* shows, there has been a significant shift from manual to non-manual occupations. We are therefore becoming by definition a more middle-class society, partly through increased social mobility, partly through the decline of manual jobs and the growth of white-collar ones. As the commentary from the 1985 *Social Trends* explains:

'Between 1971 and 1981 the proportions in Social Classes I and II combined increased from 23 per cent to 29 per cent for men and from 17 per cent to 22 per cent for women while the proportions in the manual social classes declined from 62 per cent to 56 per cent for men and from 43 per cent to 36 per cent for women.'

However this official classification of Britain's class structure has been extensively criticised on two main grounds – its reliability and its validity.

Reliability

Criticisms here centre round the accuracy with which people have been allocated to a particular social class category. First, there have been simple mistakes made by the census coders or people have misunderstood the job titles in the census form or exaggerated their own occupation and so promoted themselves up the social scale. Second, there have been criticisms of the categories themselves. Why, for example, are chorus girls and farmers in the same class, and surely there should be some distinction between the Commissioner of the Metropolitan Police and an ordinary bobby? It's nice to note that Cabinet ministers promoted themselves in 1981 from social class II to I! Third, with revisions only every ten years it is difficult for

Table 4.1 Population:[1] by social class, 1981
Great Britain

	professional	intermediate	skilled non-manual	skilled manual	semi-skilled manual	unskilled manual	Total (= 100%) (thousands)
			Social class				
Males							
Economically active	5.8	22.5	11.8	36.5	17.0	6.4	14,736
Retired or permanently sick	3.4	19.8	12.3	33.1	22.2	9.3	2,644
Females							
Married (own class)[2]	0.9	21.2	37.4	8.2	23.4	8.8	6,440
Married (husband's class)[3]	6.0	24.7	11.2	36.3	16.5	5.4	11,986
Single, widowed, or divorced	1.3	21.4	42.3	10.1	20.4	4.4	3,982
All people classified in their own right	3.8	21.8	22.2	25.8	19.5	7.0	27,803
Economically active or retired heads of households	5.4	24.8	14.2	32.1	17.4	5.9	15,321

[1] Aged 16 or over. Figures in the total column exclude people who are not classified to any particular social class.

[2] Economically active, retired, or permanently sick by own class.

[3] Married women with husbands economically active, retired, or permanently sick. Some women are classified by both their own and their husband's class, so appear twice in the table.

Source: Population Census, 1981, *Office of Population Censuses and Surveys*. (Crown copyright: reproduced with permission of the Controller of HMSO.)

this official classification to keep up-to-date with the changing status of many jobs and occupational groups, especially that greyest of boundaries between skilled manual workers and the lower middle class. Fourth, despite official disclaimers the RG scale is based on an underlying bias towards the middle class. By ranking non-manual occupations above manual ones it at least implies the superiority of brain over brawn. Finally this official ranking ignores or underestimates certain groups. The self-employed, unemployed, and retired are classified by their last job or left out and so in a sense made invisible.

Validity

Criticisms here are more fundamental and theoretical. They centre on the very basis of the official classification and its underlying assumptions.

Weberian writers generally accept the idea of occupation as a basis for class analysis but a limited one. First it ignores other sources of social stratification such as power, gender, and race. Second, it only identifies objective factors, leaving out in their view the crucial dimension of subjective class–class 'consciousness'. Having a non-manual job is only one step to being middle class. You have to feel part of it too. Studies like Goldthorpe and Lockwood's (1968) of the working class and Ken Roberts *et al.* (1977) of the middle class have shown how such class consciousness fragments as well as unites social class groupings. Roberts, for example, identified four types of middle class on this basis and Lockwood three types of working-class consciousness.

Feminist writers have highlighted the male bias behind the RG scale such that women are rendered invisible and dependent on men for any form of social status. Traditionally it was officially assumed that the husband or father was the head of the household and that his wife (and children) should be classified according to his occupation. As even the official commentary in the 1975 *Social Trends* acknowledged, this tended to concentrate married women in social class IIIM but single, widowed, and divorced women in IIIN – i.e. such a system of classification tended to downgrade most women. (This feminist critique of official statistics is more fully developed later.)

Marxist writers go even further. They reject the whole structure of the RG system. For them the real basis of the concept of social class is not occupation but the ownership and non-ownership of the means of production, and the exploitative relationships that result. For them there are only two real social classes, the bourgeoisie and the proletariat, and far from class merely being a form of social ranking, it is a reflection of an underlying class struggle that will eventually lead to social revolution, the overthrow of capitalism, and the establishment of a classless society. Like Weberian writers Marxists also emphasize class consciousness, not as a divisive influence but as one uniting the proletariat (which will increasingly include in its ranks many of the middle classes) in their revolutionary mission. Thus for them the RG scale totally fails to capture the essence of social class.

First it almost totally ignores the bourgeoisie, those that both own and control capitalist societies. The RG scale only describes occupations. It therefore only measures the middle and working classes. It leaves out those who own the means of production – land, capital, factories – and doesn't even mention the British upper class.

Second, it fragments social classes into 5–6 categories, emphasizing their differences rather than their common cause. By using status it helps justify class inequalities as natural, just, and commonly agreed. It thus acts as an 'ideological' device diverting attention from the true nature and causes of inequality and exploitation in capitalist society. It can be, and has been, used (e.g. in the *Black Report*, 1982) to identify class differences in life chances but it makes them appear inevitable or minor. It encourages acceptance of a hierarchial social structure, of brain being superior to brawn and of social mobility being a truly open avenue for the rise of the talented, ambitious, and hard working. It thus hides the self-perpetuating nature of our class system and the way the working class are kept in their place and made to accept it as right and just.

Thus for Marxists the RG scale, though occasionally useful, is essentially a descriptive not an analytical device. It ignores the economic elite who control capitalist societies, ignores the essential dynamic of social change, and juxtaposes not the bourgeoisie and proletariat but middle and working-class 'workers'. Thus in their view it is an ideological device for obscuring the class struggle, exploitation, and inequality, and for promoting class divisions and the general acceptance of capitalist values of self-interest and competition. Their vision of social class is thus very different to that of the Registrar General and their theories predict not greater social mobility but increased class conflict and eventually revolution.

Thus the official version of the concept of social class has come in for extensive criticism for both its inaccuracies and for using occupation as its prime indicator. However in its defence the RG scale was never devised as a tool of social analysis. It originated from the work of T.H.C. Henderson, a medical statistician at the Register Office who in 1911 tried to measure social class differences in mortality. It has since been used by officials for administrative purposes to classify the 'working population' into status groupings or categories of skill. It was only ever intended to be descriptive and by definition officials are bound to have a conservative rather than radical view of the social system, to be defending rather than criticizing their boss, the state. Rather officials could argue that it is sociologists who have misused it by trying to make more profound use of it than it was designed to achieve. And as writers like Martin Bulmer (1978) and Ivan Reid (1981) argue, despite all its weaknesses, occupation and the RG scale is the best indicator of social class at present available.

REID?

Activity

Now it is your turn to design a social indicator and we will give you a choice. Pick either *education* or *health* and explain exactly how you would measure the standard of education or health in Britain today using the following guidelines.

Think out your *definition* carefully – what exactly *is* health or education? Is health simply the absence of illness, or is it something much broader and more positive as in the World Health Organisation's definition that health is 'a state of complete physical, mental, and social well-being'? Is education simply what is learnt and tested at school and college or is it more than just *formal* learning?

Decide what characteristics you would *measure* or use as your standard (note how this depends on your definition). Would you simply use statistics on ill-health and death rates (and if so which ones?) or indications of physical, mental, and social well-being? Is formal education best measured by exam results (and if not why not?) and what other statistics might indicate standards of learning?

What official statistics are readily available on either of these topics? How reliable, how valid are they? What *unofficial* statistics are available? What gaps might you have to fill with your own survey and how you would design and organize it?

Further reading

The best and most readable introduction here is Ivan Reid's study, now in its second edition (1981).

5

Suicide and crime – exercises in validity

Introduction

Our discussion on social indicators touched on the key issue of the social meaning of official statistics. In this section we delve into this topic much more deeply by discussing two particular forms of deviancy – suicide and crime.

Suicide

The act of taking your own life would seem to be a purely individual act, more of interest to the psychologist than the sociologist. However if you look closely at *Figure 5.1* below certain distinctly social patterns do emerge.

- First, more men kill themselves than women.
- Second, suicide rates in recent years have fluctuated sharply. After reaching a post-war peak of 5,714 in 1963,

Figure 5.1 Suicides by sex, England and Wales, 1950–82

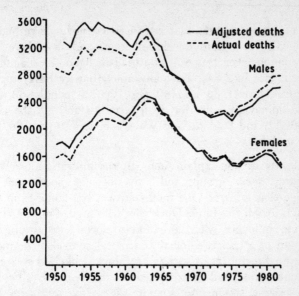

Source: OPCS *Population Trends* 35, Spring 1984. (Crown copyright: reproduced with permission of the Controller of HMSO.)

the total number of suicides for both men and women fell to an all-time low of 3,693 in 1975 but has since risen steadily to nearly 5,000 today. Though significant, such figures represent less than 1 per cent of total deaths per year in the UK – although many, many more attempt suicide (20,000 in 1983).

• Third, more detailed statistics reveal further social influences.

As Edwin Stengel has summarized it:

'suicide rates in the west have been found to be positively correlated with male sex, increasing age, widowhood, single and divorced state, childlessness, high density of population, residence in big towns, a high standard of living, economic crisis, alcohol consumption, history of a broken home in childhood, mental disorder, and physical illness.'

(Stengel 1964)

● Fourth, it appears that advanced countries have higher suicide rates than developing ones and that there are variations even between industrialized nations. Communist countries like East Germany and Hungary have suicide rates of over 36 and 40 per 100,000 population, the Scandinavian countries of between 20 and 30, the USA 10–12, and England and Wales a mere 8–9 per 100,000 population.

But how do you explain such patterns and variations? Why are some social groups and some societies more prone to suicide than others? One major answer has come from the French sociologist Emile Durkheim who argued in 1897 that the key influence was the extent of social integration, the strength of a society's social and moral controls. The more integrated members of society are, the less likely they are to commit suicide, and he expressed this theory in the following very precise statement: 'suicide varies inversely with the degree of integration of the social groups of which the individual forms a part' (Durkheim 1970). Thus for example the old, single, and divorced are more prone to committing suicide than the young and married because they are more isolated; suicide rates are higher in urban areas than in rural ones because the social controls are weaker in towns and cities; Catholics are less likely to commit suicide than Protestants because their religious rules are stricter and their rituals more communal.

However Durkheim's analysis was not simply about suicide. He was also trying to prove that social reality is essentially the same as nature, governed by similar forces and so amenable to scientific method. He therefore hoped to be able to identify the key forces controlling human behaviour and so gain for sociology the academic status of a true science. He hoped to lay the basis for a *positivist* or scientific approach to the study of society and chose suicide because if he could prove that social forces or social facts existed here then they must exist everywhere. He therefore declared that far from suicide being simply an individual act, 'there is for each people [society] a collective force of a definite amount of energy impelling men to self-destruction', i.e. its degree of social integration determines its rate of suicide.

Though a masterpiece of sociological analysis, Durkheim's study has been criticized on two main grounds.

Fellow-positivist writers, whilst agreeing with his general scientific approach, have highlighted weaknesses in the reliability of the official statistics he used. At the turn of the twentieth century such statistics were collected in a very haphazard manner, usually by priests without a medical examination, and the officials involved were constantly changing the way they were tabulated. Even modern official suicide statistics are not totally reliable. As McCarthy and Walsh (1966) showed in their study of Dublin the real rate of suicide may well be twice the official one. But what all such writers believe, whatever their differences over the amount of error in the official statistics, is that there is a real suicide rate if only they can devise an accurate enough measuring instrument to record it.

Phenomenological writers reject both the idea of scientific sociology and the positivist view of social reality. They challenge the validity of official statistics. They see society as fundamentally different to nature and human behaviour as internally governed rather than externally caused. For such sociologists society has no reality of its own, rather it is created and recreated daily by people's interactions and mutual expectations. There cannot therefore be real and objective social facts which can be measured and scientifically analyzed, only social concepts which depend for their existence on the *meaning* the people of a particular society or culture give them in a particular situation. Thus whilst Durkheim talked of all forms of self-death as suicide, phenomenologists argue that the only thing that distinguishes

57

suicide from murder, martyrdom, or an accident is *motive*. To be a true suicide the victim must have deliberately killed himself – and have done so out of despair. But since the victim is dead we cannot know his true motive, only surmise it from the evidence available, and here we ask an official called a coroner to make this social judgement or interpretation. He looks for clues that the victim's death was premeditated – a suicide note, the mode, location, and circumstances of the death, the victim's state of mind and background. However such evidence is purely circumstantial and could just as easily point to an attempted suicide as a real one. As the following example shows it may simply have been a cry for help that went wrong:

> 'A woman took a considerable quantity of barbiturate tablets at 4.30 p.m. and fell asleep on the kitchen floor in front of the refrigerator. She knew that every working day for the last three years her husband came home at 5 p.m. and went straight to the refrigerator for a beer. There was thus a strong possibility that she would be rescued. However, her husband was delayed and did not reach home till 7.30 p.m.'
>
> (Atkinson 1978)

Moreover the coroner is not only influenced by the evidence but by the reaction of others, especially the victim's family who may or may not bring pressure to protect the family name.

Thus phenomenologists like Maxwell Atkinson (1978) and Jack Douglas (1967) argue that far from suicides being social facts – predetermined, prepackaged and indisputable – as positivists seem to claim, they are social concepts created by the meaning a particular society confers on a particular form of self-death and are determined not by mysterious outside social forces but by the interpretations of an official called a coroner. Atkinson's research moreover revealed that far from resting on any scientific expertise, coroners' verdicts rest largely on common-sense or popular ideas about what a

58

typical suicide looks like. Such a stereotyped image guides his search for clues and his analysis, and if the evidence doesn't fit then he is likely to record an open verdict or accidental death. Yet his verdict *creates* another official statistic of suicide, and it is these facts and figures that both academic experts and the police use for their theories of suicide – theories that coroners occasionally read to reinforce their original stereotype! Thus a sort of self-perpetuating cycle of shared definitions and interpretations is generated by which coroners prove themselves right. imp

Thus from a phenomenological perspective the official statistics on suicide are more a reflection of the attitudes and behaviour of *officials* than of those who kill themselves, and the variations between social groups and different countries simply reflect different social definitions and different official attitudes. The high rates of suicide in advanced countries compared to poorer ones (or urban areas compared to rural ones), for example, may simply reflect their more efficient medical and judicial administrations – we in the West have more professional coroners than countries like India. Similarly Atkinson *et al.* (1975) explained the different suicide rates in Denmark and England and Wales simply by the fact that even when they are given exactly the same cases to judge, Danish coroners are more likely to return a suicide verdict than their English counterparts because, under Danish law, it is not necessary to find evidence of 'suicidal intention'. Thus whilst positivists look for the social causes behind the suicide statistics, phenomenologists have investigated the statistics themselves, how they were defined and collected, and so produced a very different picture of what official statistics really mean. NB

What Atkinson and Douglas were also trying to do – like Durkheim – was to prove that their particular perspective on society and sociological method (phenomenology) – was correct. The crucial differences between a positivist and a phenomenological view of official statistics are even more clearly revealed by our next topic – crime.

AUTOMATICITY

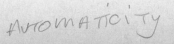

Table 5.1 Notifiable offences[1] recorded by the police: by type of offence

England and Wales, Scotland, and Northern Ireland

Thousands

	England and Wales[2]			Scotland			Northern Ireland		
	1971	1982[2]	1983[2]	1971	1982	1983	1971	1982	1983
Notifiable offences recorded									
violence against the person	47.0	108.7	111.3	5.0	7.8	8.9	1.4	3.0	3.0
sexual offences	23.6	19.7	20.4[5]	2.6	5.0	5.5	0.2	0.4	0.4
burglary	451.5	810.6	813.4	59.2	106.3	108.5	10.6	21.0	21.3
robbery	7.5	22.8	22.1	2.3	4.2	4.2	0.6	1.9	1.9
theft and handling stolen goods	1,003.7	1,755.9[4]	1,705.9[4]	104.6	209.9	207.6	8.6	26.4	27.7
fraud and forgery	99.8	123.1	121.8	9.4	22.1	24.2	1.5	2.7	2.8
criminal damage	27.0[3]	417.8[3]	443.3[3]	22.0[7]	66.0[7]	73.1[7]	7.4[7]	4.0[7]	4.6[7]
other offences	5.6[4]	3.8	8.7[6]	5.9	13.7	15.9	0.5	2.7	2.3
total notifiable offences	1,665.7[3]	3,262.4[3]	3,247.0[3,5,6]	211.0[7]	435.1[7]	447.8[7]	30.8[7]	62.1[7]	64.0[7]

[1] Offences which in 1978 and earlier years were 'indictable'. Scottish figures of 'crimes' have been recompiled to approximate to the classification of notifiable offences in England and Wales. However, because of differences in the legal system, recording and counting practices, and classification problems, Scottish figures are not strictly comparable with those for England and Wales.
[2] Figures for 1982 and 1983 are not precisely comparable with those for 1971 because of changes made by new counting rules which were introduced at the beginning of 1980.

[3] The 1982 and 1983 figures include offences of criminal damage value £20 or less; there were 176,057 cases in 1983. Such offences are excluded in 1971.
[4] Offences of 'abstracting electricity', of which there were 5,688 cases in 1983, are included among 'other offences' in 1971 and 'theft and handling stolen goods' in 1982 and 1983.
[5] Includes offences of 'gross indecency with a child' (511 offences), recorded only from the beginning of 1983.
[6] Includes offences of 'trafficking in controlled drugs' (4,994 offences), recorded only from the beginning of 1983.
[7] Includes all cases of criminal damage recorded by police.

Source: Criminal Statistics, Home Office, Scottish Home and Health Department, Northern Ireland Office.

Further reading

The best short overview here is J.M. Atkinson's essay in Stan Cohen's book *Images of Deviance* (1971).

Crime

The official statistics on crime show in particular just how important the actions of the officials involved (especially the police) and the public are in creating official statistics. They give the opportunity, too, to examine the very different interpretations different sociological perspectives have put on such figures.

The official *crime statistics* are collected by the Home Office and published in an annual volume called *Criminal Statistics: England and Wales*. In it crimes are divided into two main types: indictable (or serious) ones like murder and robbery that are usually tried by a jury, and summary (or less serious) ones such as motoring offences that are usually dealt with in a magistrates' court. The main indictable offences for 1971 to 1983 are shown in *Table 5.1*.

The total number of serious crimes in 1983 was 3¼ million with theft and handling of stolen goods at the top of the list and sexual offences at the bottom. There were 1,685,000 summary offences in 1983 of which 1.2 million were motoring offences, a slight increase on 1982. Overall the total number of offenders found guilty or cautioned in 1983 was 2,260,000, about 13 per cent higher than 1973. As the table illustrates, over the past ten to twelve years there seems to have been a crime explosion with several notifiable offences doubling, even trebling. The crime *rate* has similarly exploded from about 1,000 notifiable offences per 100,000 population in England and Wales in the mid-1950s to 6,500 in 1983.

However a closer inspection reveals, first, important differences *between* crimes and, second, that much of this boom is in less serious offences. So for example despite all the media attention they get, crimes of homicide which includes murder, manslaughter, and infanticide only totalled 550 offences in all in 1983 – a fall of 65 on 1982. Of this total 132 people were eventually convicted of murder, a fall of 52 on the 184 convictions in 1982. There were 1,300 rapes and 17,100 offences of arson in 1983 out of the total figure of 3¼ million serious offences in that year. As *Social Trends* 1985 points out, 'over 95 per cent of offences recorded by the police in 1983 were offences against property and many of these were comparatively trivial'. Theft and handling of stolen goods accounted for just over half of all recorded offences, while burglary accounted for another quarter.

The total number of serious crimes in 1983 was one per cent less than in 1982. There were falls in recorded burglary, robbery, fraud, and forgery. Similarly, of the total number of offenders found guilty in all courts in England and Wales in 1983 (2.1 million), nearly half a million were convicted of indictable offences and the rest of summary offences of which 1.2 million were motoring charges. As the 1983 *Criminal Statistics* concludes, 'The rise in the total number of offenders found guilty between 1982 and 1983 was largely due to the number of summary non-motoring offences'. In addition 165,000 people were *cautioned* by the police, 8 per cent more than in 1981. Thus the growth of crime today is not quite so serious as it first seems. What has gone down somewhat on previous years, though, is the *clear-up rate* – 'the number of offences cleared up by the police during a year expressed as a percentage of the offences recorded by the police in that year' from 45 per cent in 1971 to 37 per cent in 1983. However this too varies enormously from crime to crime. For example in 1983 whilst only 24 per cent of recorded robberies and 13 per cent of 'theft from the person' were cleared up, 75 per cent of crimes of violence against the person were, 93 per cent of homicides, and 99 per cent of handling stolen goods.

Even these figures, though, almost pale into insignificance compared to many other Western countries, not least America. As the famous criminologist Sir Leon Radzinowicz summed it up: 'There are as many murders in Manhattan each year as in the whole of England and Wales; and Houston is even worse than Manhattan. Detroit, with much the same population as Northern Ireland, has even in these grim days five times the murders' (Radzinowicz and King 1979). Nevertheless crime in Britain is serious and as the figures for 1984 (just released) show, it continues to grow. There were 3½ million crimes in 1984 and the clear-up rate fell to 35 per cent.

The typical criminal that emerges from such official statistics, especially for the more 'popular' crimes of theft, robbery, criminal damage, and violence against the person is 'young, male, working class and living in a city', with black youths being more at risk than white youngsters. Traditionally positivist writers have sought to explain such patterns of criminality in terms of socialization, male aggression, working-class failure at school, and the opportunities for crime that exist in today's anonymous cities. Robert Merton (1968), for example, proposed the theory of 'anomie', of crime being an alternative avenue to the Great American Dream of wealth and fame. Albert Cohen (1955) and Walter Miller (1962) have talked of juvenile sub-cultures and the Chicago sociologists of the 1920s claimed that inner-city areas 'bred' crime. As with suicide statistics, there is a general acceptance of official statistics (warts and all) as a relatively reliable and valid picture of crime today and a general attempt to explain it in terms of external social forces be they unemployment, lack of opportunity, or upbringing.

But just as with our discussion of suicide, phenomenologists have concentrated on the way official statistics are *created* and interpreted and in particular on the attitudes and behaviour of the officials involved. As such studies reveal, the creation of an official crime statistic is a long process involving many social actors.

Step 1: Reporting of crime

The first stage is that a crime has to be discovered and reported and the key actor here is the *public*. Over 80 per cent

63

of all crime reports come from members of the public who have identified a situation or act as criminal and reported it. However, as many studies have revealed, only a tiny proportion of crime – possibly as low as 15 per cent (20 per cent according to Radzinowicz and King (1979)) – is actually reported. This Dark Figure of Crime, as the unreported majority is called, exists because, for a variety of reasons – fear, triviality, apathy, etc. – people do not consider it worth reporting. Even official and public institutions such as schools, shops, or banks often prefer to handle the matter themselves, partly out of convenience, partly to protect their reputation.

However in the last twenty or thirty years the public seem to have become less tolerant of crime and more willing to report it. This increase in communication has been helped by:

- the spread of the telephone making reporting easier;
- the spread of insurance, especially on cars, which requires a police report before a claim can be made;
- the spread of modern organizations which have procedures and the legal obligation to report serious offences;
- improved police – public relations – the public has more faith in the police today and this leads to the ironic situation that the more effective the police are, the more crime the public report and so their clear-up rate falls and they look less efficient. From this point of view too an increase in the crime rate may not reflect a real increase in crime but simply more people reporting it.

Step 2: Recording of crime

The second stage involves the main crime officials – the police. They *record* public reports as crimes, but even this apparently simple process is complicated. The officer involved has to decide whether the offence is serious enough to record and if so under what category. Imagine trying to decide between a burglary in a dwelling and an aggravated burglary

64

Figure 5.2 How crime is 'discovered'

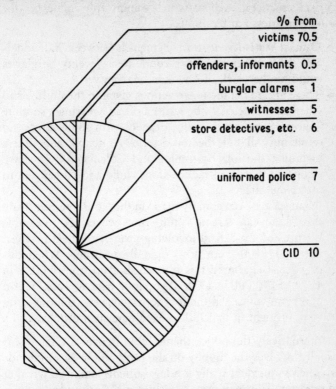

% from
victims 70.5

offenders, informants 0.5

burglar alarms 1

witnesses 5

store detectives, etc. 6

uniformed police 7

CID 10

Source: David Steer: *Uncovering crime: the police role*, HMSO, 1980. (Reproduced with permission of the Controller of HMSO.)

in a building other than a dwelling; or between an unlawful assembly and a rout. Moreover as *Criminal Statistics* itself points out, where there is doubt about the classification of an offence the police have tended to record it as the more serious offence because whilst the courts can reduce a charge they cannot increase it. Inevitably this means the official picture of crime often appears more serious than it really is.

In addition there is a whole range of administrative and clerical practices, each of which significantly influences the crime statistics. For example:

- Official statistics do not distinguish between individuals and the number of crimes committed. Twenty burglaries could be the work of one man or twenty.
- There are no detailed instructions given to the police as to when an offence is to be written off as 'no crime', so there is great variation in police practice with some forces 'no crime-ing' all but the most serious offences and others including the lot. Bottomley and Coleman (1981) have estimated that this practice alone could add 10 per cent to the crime rate.
- Changes are occasionally made in the 'counting rules' and this alone can 'create' mini-crime waves. For example offences of vandalism involving property valued between £20 and £100 were not originally recorded. When this practice was altered this offence shot up from 42,000 in 1972 to 140,000 in 1978. If you look back to *Table 5.1* on p. 60 you will see in the footnotes that new counting rules were brought in in 1980 to overcome such problems.

Alternatively the police themselves discover a crime. This usually involves the 'bobby on the beat' and he has to decide whether an incident really is a legal offence and if so whether to report it. This may seem a fairly straightforward procedure but studies in America in particular have revealed various social influences on this decision – for example, pressure from superior officers to get results or pressure by the local people to crack down on juveniles. However, the key influence appears to be the offender's *demeanour* and whether he/she fits the police *stereotype* of a typical criminal. Juveniles who act tough and show a lack of respect are more likely to be pulled in than those who are suitably polite and well-dressed. The police tend to concentrate their attention on certain social groups (and certain social areas, in particular the inner city). The 1983 Policy Studies Institute study of the Metropolitan

Police, for example, revealed that out of an estimated 1½ million 'stops' of the public by the police in a year, only 8 per cent produced a detected offence and 3 per cent a prosecution. Young men, blacks, the unemployed, and known 'villains' were the groups most likely to be stopped (as were car owners). As Aaron Cicourel (1976) has argued, the police tend to select out certain types as potentially criminal, and such selective policing produces a self-fulfilling prophecy because these social groups are then more likely to become official crime statistics and so prove the police's stereotype correct.

Step 3: Court procedures

The third stage is the courts – again an apparently straight-forward and impartial process, but again one that involves the actions and attitudes of a range of social actors (judges, solicitors, and the public sitting on juries) making social and moral judgements about whom to select out for punishment and whom to return to society. Moreover our courts are an enormous administrative system processing over two million cases a year and so short-cuts are occasionally used. One major one, in America at least, is 'plea-bargaining', where in return for a 'guilty' plea the defendant has his charge and so his sentence reduced. Whilst this saves the courts time and money on trials, it can and does lead to miscarriages of justice. Donald Newman's (1956) study in America showed, for example, how the guilty can use this system to get lighter sentences whilst the innocent get frightened into 'admitting' guilt. Even British judges and magistrates are not immune to the pressures of public opinion and as the crime rate has continued to rise they have noticeably increased sentences to the point where our prisons are now overpopulated to the tune of 51,000 inmates (1983).

Step 4: Political influences

Fourth, there are the *politicians*. They make the laws that define social behaviour as criminal and create mechanisms to

67

like those below

enforce them. They too can influence the crime statistics simply by making new laws (such as those on seat belts or picketing) or by abolishing old ones (such as those on abortion or homosexuality). Their campaigns on 'law and order' similarly put pressure on the police to prosecute and on the public to report crime.

Step 5: Media influences

Finally there are the *media* whose campaigns and headlines, like those below, not only fuel public awareness and reporting of crime but their images of it:

'BLACK CRIME: THE ALARMING FIGURES'

'LONDON'S STREETS OF FEAR'

'ON BRITAIN'S MOST BRUTAL STREETS'

(Muncie 1984)

Such headlines often distort the true picture of crime and greatly increase public fear. As John Muncie (1984) has argued, the main target for such media campaigns have been young males (especially blacks) although, as we pointed out earlier, most juvenile crime is relatively trivial. Crimes like 'mugging' (itself a media invention rather than official category) and football hooliganism have always existed yet through extensive media attention they have become *the* crimes of the 1970s and 1980s, which has led in turn to new laws and new punishments like the 'short, sharp shock'.

Thus two main conclusions may be reached about official crime statistics:

- That the fluctuations in the crime figures may well be due *not* to real increases in criminal activity but to changes in the behaviour of officials, ranging from the police to politicians, and in reporting by the public.
- That official statistics are only the tip of the crime iceberg and an unrepresentative one at that: one which reflects

police stereotypes of the 'typical' criminal rather than the typical criminal him/herself.

The Dark Figure of Crime

It is concerns like these that have led researchers to try to probe deeper and deeper into the Dark Figure of Crime. The two main attempts to do this have been:

(a) Self-report studies – confidential questionnaires circulated to samples of youngsters asking them to record any crimes they themselves have committed. Such surveys have revealed that far from being a minority activity juvenile crime is quite widespread, 'normal' even. Up to 90 per cent of youngsters interviewed admitted some form of 'delinquency' from petty theft to joy-riding. However as critics have pointed out some of these surveys included so many trivial offences that inevitably almost everyone was included, and whilst they may reveal something about juvenile crime they tell us little about more serious offences. (See *Figure 5.5* for an example of a self-report questionnaire.) NB

(b) Victim surveys. These have attempted to overcome such problems, they have tried to reach all sectors of the public and they too have revealed a wealth of unreported crime. Even the Home Office has now recognized the importance of this technique and in 1982 undertook its own *British Crime Survey* involving a national sample of 16,000 households and achieving a response rate of 80 per cent. *Good rate*

The *BCS* uncovered:

'Some six million incidents involving theft; two and a half million incidents of vandalism (or criminal damage); half a million incidents involving some form of violence (wounding, sexual offences and robbery); and a further one and a half million incidents of 'common assault'. The survey also indicated around a million incidents involving threatening behaviour, while 10 per cent of households believed that milk bottles had been stolen from their doorstep at least

69

once in the year – making this one of the most common, if least serious, single crimes in Britain today.' Don't know it

The *BCS* also revealed:

- A significant and serious underestimate of the true rate of crime in the official crime statistics as illustrated in the following chart (*Figure 5.3*).
- A significant and serious under-reporting of crime *to* the police, especially in such areas as vandalism (22 per cent), theft in a dwelling (18 per cent), and even in incidents of violence (60 per cent).
- A significant and serious under-recording of offences *by* the police, including a third of offences involving damage to property and over half involving violence. Bottomley and Coleman (1981) have called this the 'Grey Area of Crime'.
- That the typical *victim* is in fact very much like the typical criminal – not old, female, and wealthy but male, young, single, a heavy drinker, and involved in assaulting others.
- That the fear of crime is greater than the reality. Crime is a minor risk in most people's lives (outside the inner city).

On this basis, and assuming that the rates remain at 1981 levels, the survey showed that a 'statistically average' person aged sixteen or over can expect:

- a robbery once every five centuries (not attempts);
- an assault resulting in injury (even if slight) once every century;
- the family car to be stolen or taken by joy-riders once every sixty years;
- a burglary in the home once every forty years.

The *British Crime Survey* therefore concluded that not only did the Dark Figure of Crime really exist but that official statistics were both an undercount and unreliable for the sorts of reasons given above.

In all, then, official figures alone offer an unreliable

measure of crime; a fuller assessment of 'real' crime trends can be made when information becomes available from victim surveys repeated over time.

The survey further argued that the popular picture fuelled by the politicians, the media, and even the police (as they campaign for more men and resources) is an exaggerated one. Most lawbreaking is petty and therefore the police would be better advised to adopt a preventive approach – to improve public and community relations – rather than the 'crime-fighter' approach that predominates. Unfortunately in an age of urban riots 'community policing' is rapidly giving way to the 'thin blue lines' of police armed with helmets, shields, and plastic bullets trying to restore order to inner-city areas.

However even victim surveys have their weaknesses. They only record crimes that have victims, not such victimless crimes as prostitution or drugs or white-collar crimes like fraud where the victim is unaware of being cheated. It relies heavily on people's memories and on their definition of an incident as a crime. Certain groups tend to be more prepared to report crime than others. Men, whites, and the middle class tend to be more prepared to report crime than women, blacks, and the working class for whom petty crime is part of everyday life. This may explain a significant under-reporting of sexual offences against women. They usually know their attacker and prefer to suffer in silence than endure the humiliation, hostility, and sexist prejudices involved in police and court procedures in sexual assault cases.

Nevertheless despite such shortcomings and biases, both self-report studies and victim surveys have greatly helped in producing a clearer picture of crime today and in revealing the complex way the criminal justice system works as it selects out a tiny minority of offenders from the mass of crime committed for eventual prosecution and imprisonment. As we have shown this is not simply a 'technical' process but one involving intense social and political pressures, evaluations, and interactions between a wide range of officials and the general public. Of the three and a quarter million reported crimes in 1983 only 576,000 offenders were found guilty or cautioned, of whom only 74,000 (16 per cent) were placed in custody. The chart on page 74 (*Figure 5.4*), taken from the report by the 1965 Presidential Commission on Law Enforcement and Administration of Justice, illustrates more dramatically how this giant sifting machine works, in this case reducing three million crimes to 100,000 prison sentences.

As the Presidential Commission concluded, 'what is known about offenders is confined almost wholly to those who have been arrested, tried and sentenced', and yet on such a basis rest a wealth of theories and public images of crime. As Sir Leon Radzinowicz (1979) argued, if the full extent of crime was ever publicly revealed it would be so vast that it would overwhelm society, the forces of law and order, and the very faith we have in the system that keeps most of us law-abiding most of the time.

Sociological perspectives on crimes

The above outline has touched on the positivist and pheno-menological viewpoints. Whilst one sought to explain crime in terms of the patterns and causes revealed in the official statistics, the other has made those very statistics and the social processes by which crime statistics are defined and collected the object of its research. Their respective pictures of crime and the typical criminal are very different. A further dimension is added by the Marxist perspective which looks at crime statistics as a reflection of power and conflict.

Marxist writers have highlighted the *class* nature of official statistics. Whilst working-class criminality is extensively recorded, 'white-collar' crime is virtually ignored although such crimes as fraud, embezzlement, and corruption are often far more serious and have even involved presidents and kings.

'Illicit gains from white collar crime far exceed those from other crimes combined. . . . One corporate price-fixing

Figure 5.3 Levels of recorded and unrecorded crime, 1981

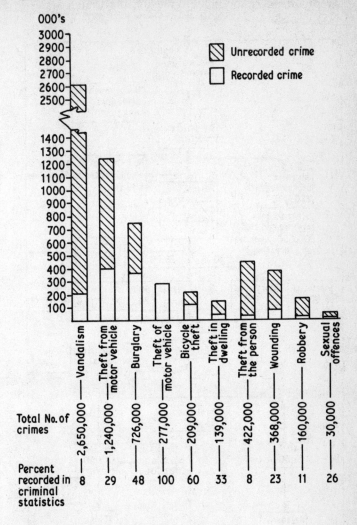

Source: Home Office Research Study (No. 76) (1983). (Reproduced with permission of the Controller of HMSO.)

Figure 5.4 Criminal justice system model (with estimates of flow of offenders for index crimes in the United States in 1965)

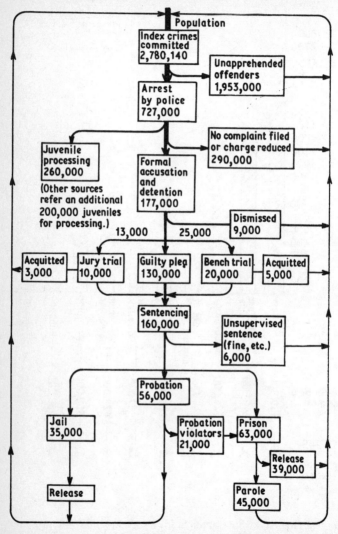

Source: Adapted from the President's Commission on Law Enforcement and Administration of Justice. *The Challenge of Crime in a Free Society* (Washington D.C.: Govt. Printing Office) in D. R. Cressey and D. A. Ward (1969): *Delinquency, Crime and the Social Process:* Harper and Row.

conspiracy criminally converted more money each year it continued than all the hundreds of burglaries, larcenies, or thefts in the entire nation during those same years. Reported bank embezzlements cost the nation ten times more than bank robberies each year.'
(Ramsay Clark 1970 (Ex US Attorney-General), quoted in Taylor, Walton, and Young 1975)

Yet such crimes are rarely prosecuted. There seems to be one law for the rich and one for the poor. It is this apparent class bias that forms the basis of the Marxist critique of official statistics which claims that, far from being neutral and impartial, such figures are part of the apparatus of physical and ideological control in a capitalist society. By portraying crime as primarily a working-class activity, official crime statistics justify the concentration of the forces of law and order on working-class areas and perpetuate the idea that crime is caused by individual inadequacy and immorality rather than by the inequalities and exploitation of the capitalist system. The ruling class can then use the law to protect their property and profits, and their control of the media to create criminal stereotypes. These fuel public outrage against sections of the working class and so justify police crackdowns on those groups who attempt to rebel against the system such as inner-city black youths. Thus in their view both the law and official statistics are part of the system of class rule in a capitalist society and only with the advent of socialism will such class control and ideological bias be eliminated.

Thus official statistics on crime are not only gathered but socially created, not only a reflection of social reality but an integral part of its daily recreation, not only a source of knowledge but part of the structure of power.

'The outcome of these processes is that the official portrait of crime and criminals is highly selective, serving to conceal crimes of the powerful and hence shore up their interests, particularly the need to be legitimated through maintaining the appearance of respectability. At the same time, crimes of the powerless are revealed and exaggerated, and this serves the interests of the powerful because it legitimizes their control agencies, such as the police and prison service, being strengthened materially, technologically, and legally, so that their ability to survey, harass, deter, both specifically and generally, actual and potential resisters to political authority is enhanced.'

(Box 1983)

It is this 'political' aspect of official statistics that forms the basis of the next section.

Figure 5.5   Self-report study

Theft less than £10
Theft greater than £10
Property destruction (<£20)
Property destruction (>£20)
Drinking alcohol
Getting drunk
Individual fist-fights
Gang fist-fights
Carrying a concealed weapon
Individual weapon fights
Gang weapon fights
Gambling
Using marijuana
Sniffing glue
Bribery involving money
Driving under the influence
Hit-and-run accidents
Cheating on exams
Using false ID
Cutting school

Activities

1. Look again at *Table 5.1* on p. 60 and answer the following questions:

(a) How many cases of burglary were there in 1971 and 1983?
(b) Which offence(s) has gone down in the period 1971–1983?
(c) What are the two major indictable offences in terms of numbers?
(d) Under which category would you include:
   - vandalism?
   - mugging?
   - rape? *serious*
   - drug trafficking? *serious*

   How to define and categorise

(e) Why are the figures for Scotland and Northern Ireland so much lower than for England and Wales?
(f) Using the footnotes explain
   - why in 1982 and 1983 the figures on criminal damage are 176,057 higher than in 1971; *rules changed*
   - why the category of theft and handling of stolen goods rose and that of other offences fell in 1982/3.

2. Look again at *Figure 5.3* on page 73 showing the results of the *British Crime Survey* and list the crimes which the official figures seriously underestimate. In what ways do surveys like this alter the official picture of the typical criminal?

3. Look at *Figure 5.5* as an example of a self-report study and try it out on the class.

Further reading

The following are very good – albeit very exhaustive – summaries of sociological research on crime:

Box (1983);
Downes and Rock (1982);
Rutter and Giller (1983) – a review done for the Home Office.

John Muncie's study (1984) illustrates the power of the media. Eileen Leonard's (1982) book is a good overview from a feminist perspective, but the best overview of crime statistics is Bottomley and Coleman's book (1981).

6

Unemployment – a case study in the economics and politics of official statistics

Introduction

Whilst suicide and crime clearly illustrate the 'social' nature of official statistics, unemployment is the classic example of their 'political' nature. The term 'political' is used here not only to refer to *party* political disputes about the size or meaning of the unemployment problem – crucial though such debates are to public understanding and general elections – but also to refer to the structure of power in our society. Official statistics themselves are part of the power of information and so whoever controls them has the power to determine not only the size of the problem but its nature, interpretation, and public image.

Moreover this topic is also part of a more fundamental debate about the nature, structure, and future of the British economy. The economy not only determines people's standard of living but their way of living, not only their lifestyle but the

Figure 6.1 Unemployment and vacancies: United Kingdom

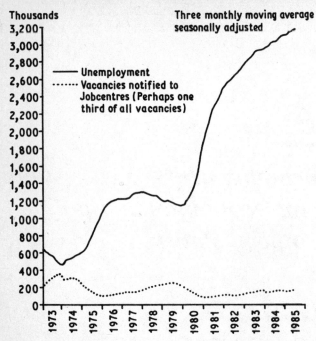

Source: Employment Gazette, July 1985. (Reproduced with permission of the Controller of HMSO.)

shape and structure of their social and political institutions; whether we can afford a welfare state or even democratic government. Periods of economic decline as in the 1930s and today threaten not only people's jobs but the social fabric. Traditional values and authority come under fire, extremist politics grow and social unrest develops. Thus the economy is the core of society and a job is an essential element of life, an important focus of meaning and a key source of stability for the individual (for men at least). Take people's jobs away and their lives begin to collapse, whole communities become ghost towns, and the very foundations of society start to rock.

Unemployment figures

As the Department of Employment statistics in *Figure 6.1* show, unemployment in the United Kingdom has grown dramatically in the last five to ten years. Though it surpassed the one million mark in the late 1970s, it has doubled, even trebled since 1979.

The 1985 *Social Trends* provides a more detailed outline of this problem:

- In September 1984 there were 3,284,000 unemployed claimants in the UK giving an unemployment rate of 13.6 per cent.
- Though most of the unemployed are male, of the total above 1,038,000 were female, 37 per cent of whom were married.
- Over 1.3 million people have now been out of work in the UK for at least a year, 760,000 for over two years and 450,000 for over three years. Among unemployed males 25 per cent had been unemployed for over two years and a further 19 per cent for between one and two years. The proportion of long-term unemployed increases with age, especially over fifty, but there is also a growing number of long-term unemployed young men (18–24) despite government schemes.
- Unemployment has predominently hit manual workers. Only 6 per cent of men in the professional and managerial groups had experienced unemployment compared to 32 per cent in the semi-skilled and unskilled manual categories.
- There are large regional variations in unemployment, with Northern Ireland the worst affected region with an average unemployment rate in 1983 of over 20 per cent, compared to the UK average of 13 per cent and to the 9 per cent rate in the south-east of England.

This is the official picture of unemployment based on official statistics. However such official figures only refer to the *registered* unemployed, to those who actually register for work and claim unemployment benefit on the day of the monthly count. Such figures do not include:

(a) The *deregistered* unemployed, those people whom officials have decided should not officially be defined as unemployed. Such groups include:

- Temporarily laid-off workers;
- Part-time workers;
- The very disabled;
- Adult students over eighteen looking for vacation work;
- School leavers;
- Those on government schemes such as YTS;
- The sick – those registered as unemployed but unavailable for work due to illness;
- The old – men over sixty who are eligible for higher long-term rates of supplementary benefit.

(b) The *unregistered* or hidden unemployed – people who are looking for work but either do not officially register for it or who cannot claim unemployment benefit, for example:

- Women – estimated by the Department of Employment as about three-quarters of this group, most of whom are married and looking for part-time work.
- Discouraged workers – those who want jobs but, recognizing the economic situation and the likelihood of getting one, do not bother registering. Again women – and older workers – make up the bulk of this group, though research in Britain and America has also identified a sizeable section of the young, especially blacks (Roberts 1983).
- The unemployable – those identified by employment officers as incapable or unsuitable for employment.
- The 'voluntary' unemployed – those not really interested in finding work, who feel better off on the dole.
- Frictional unemployment – people moving between jobs.

- The fraudulently unemployed – those registered for unemployment benefit but working 'on the side'. However even officials recognize that this is a small problem. In 1980, for example, there were only 25,000 cases of fraud, far less than one per cent of all claims made.
- The long-term unemployed – after a year of unemployment, claimants cease to be eligible for unemployment benefit. They are then only eligible for means-tested benefits for which they may not be eligible or willing to claim, so some may not bother to register. Thus as unemployment rises and the numbers of those ineligible for benefit rises, so the official unemployment figure may actually fall.

Thus unemployment statistics are a classic example of the way the definition of a social problem dramatically alters both its size and shape. By excluding or ignoring certain groups the government has managed to stabilize unemployment at about 3.3 million over the past two years. It even managed on two occasions to cut unemployment at a stroke. In 1982 Norman Tebbit, the then Minister for Employment, changed the counting rules to exclude from the official figure those who did not register for unemployment benefit. This alone cut 246,000 people from the dole queue. In 1983 men over sixty on higher long-term rates of supplementary benefit did not have to sign on at an unemployment benefit office, thus removing a further 162,000. More recently the new Minister for Employment, Lord Young, declared that the real unemployment figure was only 2.3 million because he claimed that the 1984 labour force survey showed that 200,000 of those registered as unemployed in fact had paid jobs and a further 740,000 were not seriously looking for work. At the beginning of 1986 the government 'shaved' another 55–70,000 off the official total by delaying the official count by a fortnight so as to allow for those who had found jobs to be excluded.

Alternatively it is easy to see how, by including many of the groups listed above, critics of the government have been able to claim that the true unemployment figure is four, even five million. The Unemployment Unit, for example, using the pre-1982 counting rules and including the unregistered unemployed and those on government schemes, puts the total unemployed at four and a half million. Christopher Huhne of the *Guardian*, using the LFS in a very different way from Lord Young and adding a deeper pool of 926,000 'discouraged' workers, puts the total higher at over five million.

This great statistical debate has been summed up by David Lipsey of the *Sunday Times* (6 November, 1983) as follows:

Figure 6.2 Jobless – The Great Divide
Official total: 3,094,000 (1982/3)

Left-wing critics ADD:		Right-wing critics SUBTRACT:	
Unemployed excluded by statistical changes, October 1982 (net)	189,000	School leavers	168,000
Unemployed over-sixties (no longer required to register)[1]	199,000	Claimants who are not really looking for jobs[1]	490,000
Short-time working	43,000	Severely disabled	23,000
Students on vacation	27,000	"Unemployables" – mentally or physically incapable[2]	135,000
Effect of Special Employment Measures	395,000	"Job changers" – out of work for four weeks or less	360,000
Unregistered unemployed[2]	490,000	"Black economy" workers, illegally claiming benefit[3]	250,000
Total additions	1,343,000	Total subtractions	1,426,000
TOTAL UNEMPLOYED	4,437,000	TOTAL UNEMPLOYED	1,668,000

1. Of whom 37,000 were removed between Dec 1981 and February 1982 and a further 162,000 as a result of Budget 1983 measures.
2. Estimate based on Dept of Employment survey, 1981.

1. Estimate, based on 1981 Labour Force Survey.
2. Dept of Employment estimate.
3. Unknowable: estimate based on internal government survey suggesting 8% of claims not justified.

Such statistics, however, are only one side of the 'unemployment equation'. On the other side are such factors as:

Figure 6.2 (cont.)

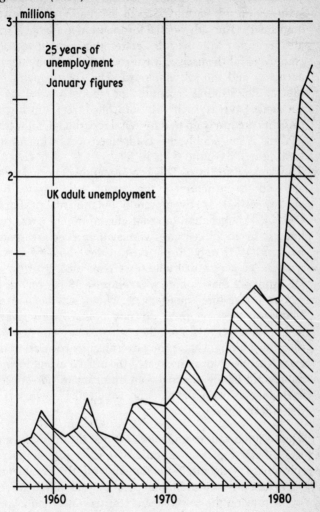

Source: CSO lagging indicator series; *Sunday Times* calculations.

- Job vacancies. Unfortunately, as the DE itself acknowledges, statistics on job vacancies, even internationally, are very inadequate. The only official information available is from jobs *registered* with the Job Centres, thus missing vacancies employers fill themselves (or through private employment agencies) and the self-employed. The DE estimates that official figures only account for about a third of all vacancies and as such jobs are filled very quickly the statistics are rarely up to date. Vital too, though, in such an analysis is not simply the availability of jobs but of jobs local people have the skills to fill.
- The demand for jobs. This is considerably affected by the age and sex structure of the labour force. As we have already seen (p. 44) the present population of working age (16–64) is larger than 'normal' due to the post-war baby booms. In addition more women than ever are seeking work. In 1921 only 30 per cent of the labour force were women, 13 per cent of whom were married. By 1991 the DE estimates that women will comprise 39 per cent of the labour force, three-quarters of whom will be married. Many of these women do not bother registering as unemployed yet it is often they who take up any new jobs that come along. Hence the government's frustration that even when new jobs are created the official unemployment figures are barely affected – an unfortunate side-effect of excluding so many people who would like to work from the official figures.

What is important to understand is that the unemployment figures do not represent a static or unchanging number of people but a constant 'flow' on and off the employment register. As many as four million people a year find themselves for some time on the employment register – nearly one in six of the entire workforce. Until recently between 250,000 and 300,000 people a month were registering for work while roughly the same amount were leaving at the same time. What is happening now is that more people are registering and fewer are leaving. Giles Merrit (1982) has described this flow as similar to a bath with water flowing in from the taps and flowing out through the plug-holes – although now there are several taps and fewer plug-holes. And over the past five years virtually all of these plug-holes or job markets, be they in manufacturing or services, have been shrinking.

Thus the key feature of the present unemployment crisis is not so much the flow of people on to the employment register but the length of time they are staying on it. In the mid 1970s the average length of stay on the dole was a fortnight. It is now approaching six months and affecting more and more people.

The most serious feature of the present situation is therefore the long-term unemployed. Over 1.3 million people have now been out of work for over a year representing 40 per cent of the unemployed, and 1 in 5 have now been unemployed for over two years.

International unemployment statistics

These are even more difficult to interpret than the British ones. Countries not only differ in their *definition* of unemployment but in the way they collect them. For example the USA includes those temporarily sick, adult students, and the temporarily laid-off, and uses its labour force survey to collect its unemployment statistics so inevitably producing a higher figure than the UK. Most countries in the OECD use a broader definition than the UK – but still have lower unemployment rates! As *Table 6.1* shows, by whatever international standard you use, the UK's rate of unemployment is one of the worst in the industrialized world.

However unemployment is a world phenomenon and it is growing. The 1983 OECD Employment Outlook Report, for example, forecast 35 million unemployed in the major industrialized countries by the late 1980s and 65–70 million by the mid-1990s. In the EEC alone there are 12.4 million unemployed today (1985) and almost 20 million in the whole

Table 6.1 *Unemployment in 16 OECD countries in 1984. Standardized % of the labour force*

	1984
high[1]	
Belgium	14.0
Canada	11.2
Denmark	10.3
Italy	10.1
Netherlands	14.0
UK	13.2
medium	
Australia	8.9
Finland	6.1
France	9.8
Germany	8.0
USA	7.4
low	
Austria	4.2
Japan	2.7
Norway	3.0
Sweden	3.1
Switzerland	1.1

[1] The limits being 10% and 5%
Source: Marxism Today (June 1985)

of Europe. But even these figures are dwarfed by unemployment in the Third World, estimated to be between 300 and 500 million and which may well reach the billion mark by the end of the century. Such figures are political dynamite. No government could publicly acknowledge them without risking not only the fall of its own government but the collapse of the world economic system. Hence possibly the official silence. As David Thomas (1985) has argued, underneath such figures is a world-wide industrial revolution shifting work from manufacturing to services.In 1961 42 per cent of the OECD workforce worked in services; today it is 60 per cent (70 per cent in the USA and Canada, 66 per cent in the UK). There has also been a great loss of jobs to the newly developing countries like South Korea and this structural change has occurred very suddenly. Britain for example lost a quarter of a million jobs in the period 1979–83 alone. But even this service sector which is mainly in the areas of welfare will only 'mop up' a limited amount of unemployment. From this perspective (although, as previously argued, national governments can make dramatic inroads into the numbers of unemployed), it is ultimately an international crisis that will require international solutions led by the USA to establish a new world order that includes the Third World and regulates such market forces. Or it will require something more radical!

The meaning of unemployment

These then are some of the facts and figures on unemployment and as you can see there is not only disagreement over what the true facts about unemployment are but conflicting opinions about what they *mean*. The official UK definition is primarily an administrative one that attempts to keep both the size and cost of the problem to a minimum. A *full* definition would be much broader and reflect its profound effects. The word 'unemployment' only dates back to the 1880s according to the *Oxford English Dictionary* and as Peter Townsend (1984) points out, total unemployment is only one extreme of a continuum that stretches from secure employment through various degrees of discontinuous employment to under- and unemployment. Similarly a full definition would include not only the impact on the individual but on his family, the local community, and the nation. It is a social, cultural, and even moral phenomenon as well as an economic one. But most of all it hits the individual. As Eisenberg and Lazarsfeld explain, the unemployed individual slips into psychological despair in three key stages:

'First there is shock, which is followed by an active hunt

89

for a job, during which the individual is still optimistic and unresigned; he still maintains an unbroken attitude. Second, when all efforts fail, the individual becomes pessimistic, anxious and suffers active distress; this is the most crucial state of all. And, third, the individual becomes fatalistic and adapts himself to his new state with a narrower scope. He now has a broken attitude.'

(Eisenberg and Lazarsfeld 1938)

Unemployment is a social disease. It breaks down both the structure and meaning of work which itself is the backbone of our present social system. Take away a man's job and you take away his sense of identity and purpose, his self-esteem, and much of his social relationships. All he is left with is the social stigma. In fact what is amazing about the present unemployment crisis is not the revolution on the streets but the lack of it. As Robert Taylor of the *Observer* explains (25 August, 1985):

'We have witnessed no riots of the unemployed. There is no national organization of the jobless. Crime, drug addiction, suicide, family breakdown and other social evils have grown, in part because of unemployment, but they have failed to make much political impression.

Why is this? A major part of the explanation lies in the characteristics of today's unemployed. They are not a static or homogeneous mass, a disciplined and self-conscious reserve army on the margins of the labour market, simply waiting to be mobilized by politicians. They constitute a constantly shifting, variegated collection of people, more than one in three of whom have not had a full-time legitimate job for over a year.'

Activities

1. • Which regions of the UK suffer from the worst unemployment and why (*Figure 6.3*)?

Figure 6.3   Unemployment rates by UK region: April 1985 (claimants only)

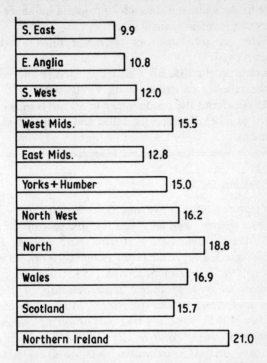

Region	Rate
S. East	9.9
E. Anglia	10.8
S. West	12.0
West Mids.	15.5
East Mids.	12.8
Yorks + Humber	15.0
North West	16.2
North	18.8
Wales	16.9
Scotland	15.7
Northern Ireland	21.0

Source: Unemployment Unit.

- Look again at *Figure 6.1* (p. 80) and try to explain the term 'seasonally adjusted'.
- Identify the groups most likely to suffer from unemployment and give two reasons for this.
2. • Explain the difference between the *deregistered* and *unregistered* unemployed. Which of the groups listed on p. 82 would you have included or excluded from an official unemployment figure and why?
- Do you consider the present official figure of unemployment to be about right, an under- or an overestimate

(look again at *Figure 6.2, p. 84*)? Give reasons to support your answer.

- Why do women have such a profound influence on the unemployment statistics?
- Why are job vacancies often not filled by the unemployed?
- Look up the official statistics on strikes and compare the number of strikes in the 1980s with those in the 1970s. Read the commentary in *Social Trends* on why the number of strikes has fallen and what such statistics mean.

Further reading

Charles Handy's book (1984) and Giles Merrit's study (1982) are both fascinating and very readable analyses of the future of work. Very helpful here is the two-part 'Society Today' article in 'New Society' called 'The Future of Work' (8 and 15 November 1985). Jeremy Seabrook (1982) uses his literary talents to evoke a profound understanding of the real meaning and effect of unemployment. Adrian Sinfield and Neil Fraser (1985) reveal the true cost of unemployment in a free pamphlet, whilst Andrew Glyn's (1984) analysis of the NCB's case against uneconomic pits raises very serious questions about the 1984 Miners' Strike and its real causes. Send for the Unemployment Unit's regular bulletins on unemployment statistics.

7

The distribution of wealth — the 'poverty' of official statistics on wealth

This case study in many ways combines all the issues so far discussed — reliability and validity, social and political influences, social knowledge. But it is also more than this. It tackles the key issue that underlies all the others, that underlies the political debate about what constitutes a just and equal society, the economic debate about how wealth should be shared, and the sociological debate about social structure and social stability. This issue is not only a philosophical and moral one but one that has inspired war and revolution, that at present separates the major political parties, divides the superpowers, and lies beneath the confrontation of capitalism and communism. To emphasize this we concentrate on the distribution of wealth rather than, as in most textbooks, on poverty alone. This helps put poverty in a much broader context, to show that the other side of mass poverty is minority wealth and that these two extremes of society are intimately related. It is also a reflection of the fact that in both these areas there is a poverty of official information. The official statistics on the poor in Britain today are very limited and fragmented. A clear picture of poverty in Britain is only really available from such unofficial sources as the Child Poverty Action Group and the Low Pay Unit. Accurate statistics on the rich are even harder to come by. Even that most meticulous of official agencies, the Inland Revenue, has trouble finding the very wealthy in our society.

It is also important to remember that not only is poverty in modern society 'relative', but so is wealth. Whilst poverty today would have been considered a reasonable standard of living in nineteenth-century Britain, so too only the very wealthy could afford a motor car or telephone fifty odd years ago.

Finally, the gap, between rich and poor is not only a financial one but a psychological one. It refers to the differences in the quality of life as well as differences in the quantity of material goods owned. Whilst a rich man may, if he is wise and chooses well, enjoy a fulfilling lifestyle of good health, education, and travel, the poor never have the freedom or opportunity so to choose. They live in a state of deprivation, for their income prevents them and their children from experiencing even the 'normal' rewards of life. The quality of their existence is poor; they are culturally, socially, and psychologically deprived, living in poor housing in a noisy and stressful environment with a lack of stimulus.

It is this gap in lifestyles and opportunities that lies behind the distribution of wealth. These three considerations make both poverty and wealth especially difficult to measure and clearly highlight the political and social nature of the figures in these fields.

The distribution of wealth

Though wealth is usually thought of purely in terms of money, in fact it is owned in such a wide variety of forms that it is extremely difficult to measure. The Inland Revenue uses two main features – personal *income* and personal *wealth* (note the difference).

Personal income

As *Table 7.1* shows, the distribution of income in the UK is very uneven. In 1981–2, for example, whilst the top one per cent received 6 per cent of total income *before* tax, the bottom 10 per cent got only two per cent; whilst the top 50 per cent shared out 75 per cent of personal income, the bottom 50 per cent received only 22.7 per cent. Moreover as a glance through the figures for 1978/9 and 1975/6 shows this inequality has increased in recent years. However as the right-hand section of the table shows, our system of taxation does help produce some redistribution of income. In 1981/2 for example the proportion of income going to the top one per cent fell to 4.6 per cent and that for the bottom 50 per cent rose to 25.2 per cent after tax.

Personal wealth

Wealth here refers to 'marketable' wealth, wealth that can be sold off and turned into income such as stocks and shares, bank and building society deposits, consumer durables, housing, and land. As *Table 7.2* shows, the distribution of wealth is even more uneven than that of income. In 1982, for example, the richest 5 per cent of the adult population owned 41 per cent of marketable wealth and the top 50 per cent controlled 96 per cent of it thus leaving the *bottom 50 per cent* with only 4 per cent to share amongst them.

However the chart does appear to show some decline in the concentration of wealth over the past ten years with the top one per cent's share, for example, falling from 31 per cent to 21 per cent in 1971–81. Second, a much more equitable picture appears when such non-marketable assets (those that

Table 7.1 Distribution of income[1] before and after tax[2]

United Kingdom

percentages and £s

	income before tax			income after tax	
	percentage share	average income (£s)	tax paid as a percentage of pre-tax income	percentage share	average income (£s)
quantile groups					
1975–6					
top 1 per cent	5.7	16,361	46.2	3.9	9,006
next 9 per cent	20.5	6,537	25.1	19.2	4,907
next 40 per cent	50.0	3,582	19.4	50.3	2,896
lower 50 per cent	23.8	1,368	9.2	26.6	1,229
1978–9					
top 1 per cent	5.3	21,819	40.0	3.9	13,172
next 9 per cent	20.8	9,501	21.9	19.5	7,442
next 40 per cent	50.4	5,171	16.6	50.4	4,307
lower 50 per cent	23.5	1,944	7.2	26.2	1,791
1981–2					
top 1 per cent	6.0	36,305	37.1	4.6	23,083
next 9 per cent	22.3	14,982	22.3	21.0	11,698
next 40 per cent	49.2	7,437	17.2	49.2	6,176
lower 50 per cent	22.7	2,725	6.2	25.2	2,526

[1] Yearly income from employment, self-employment, investment, cash benefits, and income in kind.
[2] After deduction of income tax but before deduction of national insurance contributions.

Table 7.2 Distribution of wealth

	United Kingdom						percentages and £s billion
	1971	1976	1978	1979	1980	1981	1982
(a) Marketable wealth							
Percentage of wealth owned by:							
Most wealthy 1 per cent of population[1]	31	24	23	22	21	21	21
„ „ 2 „ „ „	39	32	30	28	28	28	28
„ „ 5 „ „ „	52	45	43	40	38	40	41
„ „ 10 „ „ „	65	60	57	54	51	53	56
„ „ 25 „ „ „	86	84	83	77	76	79	81
„ „ 50 „ „ „	97	95	95	95	95	96	96
Total marketable wealth (£s billion)	140	263	369	453	529	565	602
(b) Marketable wealth plus occupational and state pension rights							
Percentage of wealth owned by:							
Most wealthy 1 per cent of population[1]	21	14	13	13	12	12	11
„ „ 2 „ „ „	27	18	17	17	16	16	16
„ „ 5 „ „ „	37	27	25	25	24	24	24
„ „ 10 „ „ „	49	37	36	35	33	33	34
„ „ 25[2] „ „ „	69–72	58–61	57–60	56–59	55–58	56–59	56–59
„ „ 50[2] „ „ „	85–89	80–85	79–83	79–83	78–82	78–82	78–82

Source: Inland Revenue in *Social Trends* (1985). (Reproduced with permission of the Controller of HMSO.)

cannot be sold off) as occupational and state pensions are added in. Thus in the bottom half of the chart the percentage of wealth owned in 1982 by the top 5 per cent is now only 24 per cent whilst that of the top 50 per cent has fallen to about 80 per cent.

This then is the official picture of the distribution of wealth and income – one of considerable inequality but also one of gradual redistribution. However such statistics – and so this picture – have been subjected to considerable criticism on two main grounds:

- First, over their 'reliability', over whether they give a full and accurate description of the distribution of wealth or significantly underestimate, even distort it.
- Second, over their validity, over whether these statistics are measuring all forms of wealth or even the most important.

Reliability

The statistics on the Distribution of Income are derived from three main sources:

- The Inland Revenue *Survey of Personal Incomes* (*SPI*);
- The Department of Employment *New Earnings Survey* (*NES*);
- The *Family Expenditure Survey* (*FES*).

However all three tend to underestimate personal income, as they tend to miss such extra incomes as part-time work and investments because of small samples and limited response rates. The most important is the *SPI* but because it only covers those with tax records, it misses those not paying tax (or avoiding it) and excludes information on benefits and such non-taxable deductions as mortgage interest, work expenses, and superannuation contributions. All three surveys are combined to form the CSO *Blue Book* series but as you can see they represent not only an underestimate of total personal income but a particular underestimate of the self-employed and higher income groups. Moreover they only refer to personal income not institutional earnings.

The Inland Revenue's estimate of the distribution of wealth is based on the estates left by those who die each year. Such estates are assumed to be a representative sample of the wealth of the living and so they are 'blown up' according to the average mortality rate of each sector of the population. This is called the Estate Multiplier Method and was explained by the Diamond Commission as follows:

> 'Thus for example, if an individual dies leaving £1,000 and the death rate of the group to which he belongs is one in twenty, the wealth of the group as a whole will be estimated at £20,000' (*Diamond Report*, no. 5, 1977: 230).

However, this method of calculating wealth has been criticized in three main ways.

First, it misses out large numbers of people with relatively small amounts of wealth.

Second, there are all sorts of ways estate duty can be avoided, ranging from gifts to relatives to investing in forestry or objects of national scientific, historic, or artistic importance. Total reliefs and exemptions on estates worth more than £50,000 cost the Inland Revenue £840 million in 1981–2.

Third, there are major problems of valuing someone's estate. For example how do you value such items as clothing or consumer durables – at their replacement cost, market value, or original price? How do you value life insurance policies which are of limited worth to someone when alive but a lot when he/she is dead? Most especially how do you value many things such as stocks and shares whose prices are continually going up and down?

To these gaps in the 'wealth' statistics add the following gaps and underestimates of 'income'.

• Tax allowances, which have grown to such an extent that through the advice of chartered accountants the rich can easily keep most of their money, especially in recent years: 'for the rich Britain has become a fiscal paradise' (Bellini 1984). Tax is now collected on less than half of gross declared income and 'perhaps only a third of total real income' argues Peter Townsend (1984). Wealth taxes (capital gains, estate duty, etc.) have never been that important and today only represent 2½ per cent of total Inland Revenue taxes. With the present government's restructuring of the tax system since 1979 only about 3 per cent of tax units now pay tax above the standard rate of 30 per cent.

• Fringe benefits, such as free company cars, free life insurances, and low interest loans are now so extensive that they can add 20 to 40 per cent extra to a top manager's pay packet (PA Personnel Services 1985).

• Tax evasion, the full extent of which is obviously unknown, has been put by Sir William Pile, chairman of the Inland Revenue, as high as 7½ per cent of GDP – equivalent to £16 billion in 1981. Such evasion is obviously easier for the rich and self-employed than for PAYE employees who have few opportunities to escape tax.

• Sources of wealth: finally it is important to remember that the wealth and income of the rich come from very different sources to those of the average and poor. For example the top five per cent rely more on investments and self-employment than employment for most of their income, whilst for most people employment is the chief source (79 per cent). In contrast the bottom 25 per cent rely on social security payments for over 70 per cent of their income (Central Statistical Office 1984). Similarly, whilst for most people their house is their major source of wealth, for the rich, land and shares are. This has a significant effect too on the distribution of wealth. Part of the apparent redistribution of wealth in the early 1970s was due to the dramatic fall in share prices – which hit the rich – and the sudden rise in house prices which benefited home-owners. Now that the values of both shares and houses have settled down again this apparent redistribution has disappeared. Similarly although *Table 7.1* made the distribution of income seem more egalitarian because of the progressive nature of *direct* taxation, it ignored indirect taxes like VAT which have a regressive effect (hit the poor more than the rich) and so balance out the gains apparently made.

The picture that emerges from this wide range of criticisms is a very different one to the official one painted on p. 95. They reveal a whole series of systematic underestimates, serious enough to show that the real distribution of wealth is probably even more unequal than that revealed by official statistics. To put such figures into a more human perspective Chris Pond (in Field 1983) estimates that the top one per cent of the adult population represents slightly more than 400,000 people – the turnout normally expected at Epsom on Derby Day! This top one per cent not only own nearly a quarter of all personal wealth but they also own almost 70 per cent of the personal wealth held in the form of land, and almost half that in the form of buildings (other than dwellings). The same one per cent of the population own 70 per cent of the listed ordinary shares and 77 per cent of the other company securities, and two-thirds of all UK government securities.

'The concentration is still more remarkable when one considers the wealth-holdings of the richest 0.1 per cent of the population. There were little more than 40,000 people in this group. But between them they owned over forty per cent of the private land, a quarter of the listed ordinary shares and a third of other company securities in private hands plus a third of UK government securities.'

(Pond, in Field 1983)

Though such figures are a fall on the 70 per cent of wealth owned by the top one per cent in 1912 they are still so extreme that for most people they are meaningless. Moreover as Playford and Pond (Field 1983) point out, wealth and income are not separate sources but feed into each other.

Similarly what redistribution of wealth has occurred has not been between the rich and the poor but, as A.B. Atkinson

(1972) put it, between the rich and the rich, from the top one per cent down to the next 4 per cent. As the Diamond Commission noted, 'if the decline of the share of the top one per cent is ignored, the shape of the distribution is not greatly different in 1976–7 to what it was in 1949'. It all depends on what is included. If, as in *Table 7.2*, state and occupational pensions are included, then a more egalitarian picture emerges, but as Chris Pond argues, if you are going to include pensions (and so make the poor and average look wealthier), why not also include private education and private health?

Statistics on the distribution of wealth are therefore extremely controversial and intensely political. Whilst it was a Labour government that set up the Diamond Commission to investigate the distribution of wealth in Britain, it was a Conservative administration that disbanded it for fear of inciting 'the politics of envy'. Moreover, official sources cannot even agree on the total amount of wealth in Britain today. Whilst the Inland Revenue put the total wealth in 1975 at £190 billion, the Diamond Commission put it at £240 billion and the Central Statistical Office at £290 billion.

Validity

Just as the reliability of official statistics in this field has been questioned so too has their validity. Radical critics, especially Marxist writers, have not only argued that the official statistics seriously underestimate the wealth of the rich but also ignore the economic, social, and political power such wealth gives. For Marxist writers, the key source of wealth and power in a capitalist society is the ownership of *capital*, the control or the means of production. It is this which determines both the total amount of wealth and its distribution; it is the private ownership of the means of production that gives capitalist societies their inegalitarian character and their extremes of wealth and poverty. Chris Hird (Hird and Irvine 1979) shows that such ownership is even more concentrated than that of 'personal wealth with the "top" 8.3 per cent owning 94.6 per cent of listed ordinary shares and 90.9 per cent of all land'. The core of economic power, though, is institutionalized and even more concentrated. Hird cites Department of Trade statistics to show that even in the period 1969–70 just over 30 insurance companies controlled 85 per cent of all insurance company assets, 40 pension funds controlled 75 per cent of all pension fund money and the Big Four Banks controlled 70 per cent of all bank deposits. Industrial ownership is similarly concentrated, as Sir Arthur Knight of the National Enterprise Board explained:

'It is too often forgotten that eighty per cent of our manufacturing industry is run by 400 firms, in each of which three or four people are responsible for the key strategic decisions – say 1500 at most. And in the investing industry (pension funds, insurance companies, etc.) I would guess that the number of key individuals is even smaller.'

(Quoted in Cripps 1981)

Thus whilst with the spread of home-ownership, pensions, and consumer durables it may appear that wealth is more widely distributed, the ownership of capital and the control of the economy have fallen into fewer and fewer hands – yet official statistics fail to reflect this. As Hird argues:

'The owners and controllers of the major means of production constitute an enormous missing area in Diamond's view of changing economic power and wealth in society. Their increasingly powerful position as controllers of capital, which is crucially different from other forms of wealth, places in their hands key decisions concerning the production, reproduction, and distribution of wealth in our society.'

(Hird and Irvine 1979)

But how is such wealth and power transmitted, how is the upper class reproduced? Here the role of the family and inheritance is crucial. As the Diamond Commission pointed out:

> 'We would need to understand the role of the family in the reproduction and transfer of wealth – a role whose significance may be gauged from the estimate that around twenty-five per cent of all wealth is inherited, with a much higher proportion among the very rich.'
>
> (*Diamond Report*, no. 5)

Big estates are often broken down into smaller ones but kept within the family. The idea that the rich are primarily self-made millionaires like Clive Sinclair and Robert Maxwell is something of a myth. Most inherited their father's fortunes and increased them. Professor Harbury found that 60 per cent of men leaving £100,000 or more since the 1950s had rich fathers. The very rich include such landed families as the Grosvenors and such business families as the Guinesses, Sainsburys, and Cadburys. Wealth begets wealth – and power. As Harbury and Hitchens (1980) concluded: 'without question . . . inheritance is the major determinant of wealth inequality'. Moreover by analyzing wealth and income only in terms of individuals the official statistics further hide both the concentration and power of wealth *within* families.

Conclusions

As the above discussion shows, measurement of both wealth and poverty hangs on the definition used. Use a limited definition, as official statistics do, and both wealth and poverty appear to be simply 'social problems'. Use a broader definition, as do radical writers, and the whole social and political structure of advanced capitalist societies is called in to question. Instead of poverty being an isolated problem caused by the inadequacies of the poor, it is now seen as a direct result of an unequal distribution of wealth. The poor are poor because the rich are rich – and determined to stay so. A radical analysis reveals the gross inequalities in income and wealth that lie beneath the apparently egalitarian picture of modern Britain painted by officials and politicians. It shows that the only real solution to modern poverty is a radical redistribution of wealth.

This is exactly what we have seen in the 1980s under the present Conservative government – not, however, a redistribution from rich to poor, but from poor to rich as part of an economic, social, even moral, programme to stimulate and reward enterprise and wealth creation. According to the Institute of Fiscal Studies (*Guardian* 18 July, 1985), 6 per cent of the British people are better off as a result of the government's tax and benefit cuts since 1979 and 87 per cent are worse off. According to Peter Townsend (1984): 'On the Government's own admission the richest ten per cent had increased their disposable incomes in real terms by £1,557 a year between 1978–9 and 1981–2, whereas the poorest twenty per cent were £82 a year poorer.'

The 'top people' in the public sector received pay rises of between 15 per cent and 46 per cent in 1985, but the average public employee only got 5–7 per cent. The low paid had their wages councils abolished and their numbers have grown to over 8 million. Whilst the power of the unions has been severely weakened by the miners' defeat in 1984, the better-off are being encouraged by further tax cuts and the prizes of privatization. Whether such policies work as intended has yet to be seen, but what is clear is that the gap between rich and poor is growing and creating new social divisions and unrest.

Activities

Look again at *Tables* 7.1 and 7.2 on pp. 96 and 97 and answer the following questions:

- Define the terms 'income' and 'wealth'.
- Define the term 'poverty'.
- What percentage of income *before* tax was owned by the

top 10 per cent of the adult population in 1981–82?
- Does our tax system help redistribute wealth and income – and if not why not?
- Why do many writers see the official figures on wealth and income as underestimates?
- What for Marxist writers is the real source of wealth in a capitalist society?
- What arguments might the present Conservative government advance for making the distribution of wealth and income more unequal?
- What arguments are there against this?
- What are your views?

Further reading

The 'blockbuster' on Poverty is inevitably Peter Townsend's massive study of 1979, though Walker, Lawson, and Townsend (1984) is more up-to-date and adds a European dimension. The pamphlets published by the CPAG reveal the grassroots effect of poverty in a simple and evocative style whilst Joan Higgin's update (1985) is a very good overview of the whole topic. David Donnison's (1982) insights on the welfare state provide a disturbing analysis of the politics of poverty.

There is very little on wealth that is relatively easy to read for students. The most accessible are Frank Field's two Wealth Reports (1979 and 1983).

8

Gender – the vital statistics on sex

Introduction

No, I am sorry if I have suddenly woken some of you up, sorry if you thought that at last this book was going to deal with some *serious* statistics, be they of Marilyn Monroe or George Michael, but I am afraid that this section is not going to be a statistical analysis of the *Karma Sutra* nor a mass of facts and figures about who does what with whom and how (if you are interested try reading the *Kinsey Report* or *Hite Report* listed in the references).

Rather this section is about women (and men), about the enormous differences in the distribution of wealth, lifestyles, and status between the sexes, as revealed (and hidden) by official statistics. It is about the structure of sexual power and the statistics of sexuality inequality. It is about the lack of information and the biased assumptions behind official facts and figures that lead to half the population of this country being almost invisible. Behind their appearance of impartiality and neutrality, official statistics reflect a distinct, consistent, and structured bias against women in two main ways:

(a) By providing statistical evidence of sexual inequalities in a range of fields;
(b) By ignoring the existence or contribution of women in many other areas.

Such ignorance is not so much deliberate as almost unconscious. It is assumed that it is unnecessary to make distinctions between the sexes. It is assumed that men, especially husbands, are quite capable of speaking for and representing women. Such assumptions reflect a structure of power and control in our society whereby men dominate women physically, politically, and ideologically both in and outside the home. Feminists call this 'patriarchy' and even official statistics contribute to it. By underplaying the role of women they make them and their needs officially invisible and reinforce the idea that it is natural for men to rule and for women to obey. Whilst many of these claims may seem rather extreme – merely feminist propaganda and a gross exaggeration – the following examples will show that this is the essence of ideological power. It is so all-pervasive and accepted as 'normal' that it is seldom questioned, and even women come to feel guilty about not fulfilling their traditional roles and being subordinate. Thus instead of women generally being kept in their place by force – in the home, at work, in bed (?) – they often do it themselves. By analyzing such an apparently neutral and innocuous area as official statistics feminists hope to reveal just how fundamental patriarchy is to our whole way of thinking.

We have touched on the position of women in a number of other areas. What this section attempts to do is draw such threads together and so encourage you to look at all statistics from a gender perspective as well as from a social and political viewpoint.

To clarify this argument consider this definition of sexism by Ann and Robin Oakley:

> 'Sexism is a type of discrimination between people based on their social classification as female or male. Such discrimination may involve behaviour, emotions, conscious attitudes and values, or the domain of unconscious ideas and assumptions. The concept of sexism is commonly used to refer to discrimination against women, but it may also be used to refer to discrimination against men (or to discrimination in favour of one sex or the other).'
>
> (Irvine, Miles, and Evans 1979)

For the Oakleys sexism is reflected in modern society by the continuing oppression of women: 'Their role as unpaid domestic producers and reproducers, their restriction to low paid and low status employment, their minimal involvement (compared with that of men) in professional occupations and in the exercise of political and economic power' (Irvine, Miles, and Evans 1979).

Such a sexual division of labour is both separate from and linked to the class divisions of modern capitalist societies. The Oakleys have gone on to identify five key ways in which sexism permeates official statistics, of which the conceptual level is the most fundamental. The conceptual scheme used in the production of official statistics embodies a particular (sexist) mode of thinking (although it also reflects institutional 'needs').

Therefore in their view official definitions are based on underlying assumptions about the traditional roles of men and women. Overwhelmingly, as Muriel Nissel (EOC 1980) argues, the focus of official statistics is on the 'male'; women and children are merely his dependents. And this has been the case since the beginning of official statistics, as the aim was only to collect taxes and armies. Government interest in statistics about women only grew with the analysis of population statistics and the crucial importance of female fertility. Though changes are now occurring, official definitions and statistics still do not put women on an equal footing with men, as the following examples illustrate.

The 'head of household'

This is the very basis of the census form and most official surveys. Since 1801 it has officially been assumed that the head of household is male and even when the spouses are of equal status official practice gives the man predominance by virtue of age. The official definition is as follows:

'The head of household is a member of the household and is, in order of precedence, the husband of the person, or the person who:

(i) owns the household accommodation or
(ii) is legally responsible for the rent of the accommodation
(iii) has the accommodation by virtue of some relationship to the owner in cases where the owner or lessee is not a member of the household.

Where two members of different sex have equal claim, the *male is taken as head of household*. When two members of the same sex have equal claim the *elder* is taken as head of household.'

As Muriel Nissel argues (EOC 1980), such a definition ignores individual differences and contributions and assumes all households have a head and that it is a man. So much for the apparently 'democratic' trend towards joint conjugal roles in nuclear families. So much, too, for the major social phenomenon of the last thirty years, the growth of 'working' wives. Thus the 1977 GHS declared three-quarters of heads of households to be male and only one quarter female, most of whom were single women (especially OAPs) and one-parent families. Likewise official surveys assume that the housewife is female, even if domestic duties are shared, and that the income she brings in is of secondary importance. The 1981 census form (see Appendix B) did acknowledge this bias by not defining the head of household so rigidly or by sex, and it included a column for 'joint' head of household.

The 'chief economic supporter'

This is again assumed to be male as the 1971 census defined it:

'1. those in full-time employment or not employed at all take precedence over part-time or retired workers;
2. married men or 'widowed or divorced persons in families' are preferred over other members of families or 'persons not in families';
3. *males are preferred over females*;
4. older persons are selected before younger.'

Reread each of these points and you will clearly see their inbuilt bias towards male 'chief economic supporters'.

Work

As Audrey Hunt argues (EOC 1980), the main statistics on economic activity are based primarily on a masculine concept of work (as a full-time, lifelong career) rather than a feminine one that fits around marriage, childbirth, part-time work, and a fragmented career. Further this conventional model only refers to *paid* employment, thus totally excluding the 'economic' contribution of about 85 per cent of all British women aged 16–64. Housewives are rather categorized as 'economically' inactive, alongside the retired, sick, and disabled (Q10, 1981 census form). Similarly as we saw with the unemployment statistics, the official definition only covers those who 'register' for work and so leaves invisible a key element in any serious analysis of unemployment and the demand for jobs.

Sickness statistics likewise depend on registration but again you can only claim if full contributions have been made, thus producing a serious underestimate of illness among women. Official statistics do show that women still only get 70 per cent of the pay of men for similar work, but even this may be an overestimate as the main source of such data – the *New Earnings Survey* – excludes private domestic service and the self-employed. Moreover by concentrating on PAYE it possibly misses the very low paid who pay no tax, amongst whom women predominate.

Social class

As already explained (pp. 50–1), married women are officially categorized by the Registrar General by their husband's social class even if they have their own occupation. As the Oakley's argue, this is an unreasonable assumption and tends to lead to the downgrading of many women (especially from social class IIIN to IIIM).

Official statistics and feminism

These then are just a few examples of sexism. There are many others and whenever you look at official statistics on crime, health, leisure activities, and so on, always now look at the way they were defined, at what the statistics tell you and what they leave out about gender differences. Many women writers now argue that there should be both more information on women's lives today – on, say, the female life-cycle of child-rearing, on the male–female distribution of income, household tasks, and even leisure – and that official definitions should be 'neutered'. However for Ann and Robin Oakley such adjustments are not enough. For them such statistical deficiencies and distortions represent more than mere male bias but an ideological framework that deliberately and systematically differentiates the sexes, conceiving of masculinity and femininity as 'opposed and contradictory' and perceiving women as a minority and subordinate group. The concerns of government are those of the 'majority' and dominant group – men. Such a bias leads not only to information on women not being collected or only partially collected but to an unsound and out-of-date conceptual model. Official statistics are still heavily based on a model in which the husband is head of the household, chief economic supporter, and dominant decision-maker, in an age when women are flocking out of the home to go to work.

Official statistics therefore are not only an inadequate reflection of the role of women today but a false one that helps preserve the image of male supremacy. Possibly, as Muriel Nissel points out, this also reflects the structure of the CSO in which it is men rather than women who create the official definitions.

Table 8.1   *Gender distribution of CSO employees*

	male		female
assistant statistician	1	:	1
senior assistant statistician	3	:	2
statistician	6	:	1
chief statistician	10	:	1
under-secretary and above	20	:	1

Source: M. Nissel in EOC (1980).

However this is not to argue that official statistics are unusable but only that they need to be handled with caution. They do contain a wealth of information on gender and this is exemplified in Eileen Wormald and Ivan Reid's fascinating book, *Sex Differences in Britain* (Reid and Wormald 1982).

Further reading

There is very little available on women and official statistics, though Reid and Wormald's analysis (1982) is an excellent and very revealing overview of gender divisions in modern British society.

PART III
Theory and method
in official statistics

9

The process of collecting/creating official statistics

Introduction

Having analyzed the technical, social, political, and sexist influences on official statistics, we now turn to a detailed examination of how they are manufactured, how they are turned from questions and answers into numbers and charts. There is, however, a certain lack of information on this process. For reasons of official secrecy or because publication of such inside information is not seen by the GSS or its agencies as worth the time and public expense involved, there is little material available on how official surveys, registrations, or the census is organized from start to finish, from deciding what data to collect through to defining, collecting, coding, analyzing, and publishing it. The appendices at the back of official volumes do certainly help by giving information on sample sizes, sampling frames, response rates, and the like, as do articles published in *Social Trends*, *Population Trends*, the

Employment Gazette, and the very useful publications and guides by the CSO. However little of this goes below the academic surface to reveal in detail such key stages as defining social variables or to clarify the problems, errors, and complications that occur even in official projects. However some information on such topics is available from academic studies, in particular those on research methods.

The collection of official statistics

As already explained, official statistics are collected in two main ways – by registration forms and by social surveys.

Registration

A stream of information pours daily into government offices from every part of Britain and many parts of the world as people officially register their births, deaths, marriages, cars, and so on. Some of this registration is direct – forms are sent directly from members of the public to the relevant government department. Some of it is indirect – reported to a public official – a policeman, coroner, doctor – who in turn decides whether to report it and under what heading. Some of this data is fed automatically to one of the GSS agencies, while other statistics are collected by individual government departments for their own use and may or may not be published.

The prime instrument for collecting all this information is the dreaded official form. If you have ever tried filling one in you will know only too well how complicated and confusing they are. Almost inevitably form-filling suffers from problems of both reliability and validity. Its problems of reliability (or inaccuracy) include:

- people failing to register or report an 'official' event;
- people failing to complete an official form properly;
- officials making mistakes in collating, coding, and analyzing completed forms;

- intermediaries like a doctor or policeman making errors and failing systematically to report all 'official' incidents.

However a more serious problem is that of validity and as we have already seen in Part II, official statistics on such topics as crime, suicide, and unemployment are often more a reflection of the attitudes, values, and behaviour of officials than of the people they claim to be representing. As we shall see the use of 'forms' increases the problems of validity because the way they are worded and structured can often lead to ambiguity and misunderstanding to the point where people are not answering the actual questions officials asked. However in processing these replies officials are often unaware of this and so assume the resultant data does reflect what people think. So bad is the problem of official jargonese that many government departments have totally rewritten and simplified their official forms.

Social surveys

These constitute the other main way in which officials collect facts and figures, and as we saw in Part I the largest and most important is the census. However they too suffer problems of reliability and validity and though we do not have the space to go into detail about each stage and source of error it is important to our discussion of the meaning of social statistics to touch briefly on some of the most important. (For a fuller discussion see the companion volume in this series – *Research Methods* by Patrick McNeill – and make especial note of the problems of *sampling*.)

The following discussion relates to both official forms and social surveys, as both have to go through the same stages and both suffer similar problems.

Definitions

This is the most crucial stage of designing a survey or official form. It determines not only what is collected but how much.

It is the key means by which the official ensures that the data he collects from the public really is what his political masters or official superiors actually wanted, otherwise they are going to be formulating official policy on a false basis. The crucial importance of this *conceptual* stage has been emphasized throughout the case studies in Part II and it feeds directly into the next stage – the design and wording of official forms.

The design and wording of official forms/questionnaires

This type of measuring or collecting instrument is based on one key assumption – that just as a miner digs up coal or a fisherman trawls for fish so an official or sociologist merely has to collect up facts and figures like shells from a seashore. This further assumes that:

- the people being questioned have got the information required;
- they are willing to part with it;
- they understand fully what is being asked of them.

Even a cursory glance at what is expected of the public – and more especially at the idea that facts and figures are lying around 'already formed' waiting to be collected – will make you realize how complicated and open to error such projects are. Crucial to this method is ensuring that the public understand what is being asked and are both willing and able to co-operate in an interviewing situation.

Question wording   As any standard research methods textbook will tell you, question wording is a highly skilled task equivalent to any other form of linguistic translation. All too easily questions may be incomprehensible, ambiguous, or biased, even when the intention was not to 'load' the question. Even the apparently simplest of words are open to misinterpretation as William A. Belson's study (1981) of the official questionnaire used in the 1959 National Readership Survey so clearly showed. In his study of twenty-nine

120

apparently straightforward questions about television viewing habits he found only 29 per cent of all respondents fully understood all of them. The highest score for any one question was 58 per cent and eight questions scored below 16 per cent. To give two very simple examples:

- The word *children* was intended to mean 'children in general'. It in fact produced 120 possible interpretations of what ages should or shouldn't be included. As Belson explained, not only did many of the respondents not include those over ten years of age but quite a lot excluded those *under* ten. Some respondents only dealt with their own children or unusual children.
- The word *household* so beloved of official forms caused less problems though a few respondents also included other families living in the same block of flats or row of houses.

As William Belson concluded, 'There is no escaping the fact that question misunderstanding is a constant threat,' and he picked out for special mention the official form: 'Perhaps the biggest offender amongst the mass media is the official "form", where an obsession with complicated expression can defeat all but those who are very determined to understand' (Belson 1981).

Recall Second, such forms and questionnaires assume people can remember the information required but, as Louis Moss and Harvey Goldstein (1979) point out, all too easily people forget or become confused over time as information 'decays' or gets overlaid by other events and memories. Much depends on how important the information was to the respondent, and even then there is the danger of it being reinterpreted in the light of hindsight or subsequent events. As even the simplest of national surveys illustrate, people forget their ages, birthplaces, and even their height, with women being more likely to shrink and men to grow.

Interviews

Having designed the questionnaire it is now necessary to get people to fill it in. Although most of the following discussion refers primarily to survey interviews, its implications are just as relevant to any form-filling situation where an official is completing the questionnaire, whether this takes place at a registry office or a Job Centre.

The major problem of all interview situations is 'interviewer bias' – the extent to which the interviewer by their appearance, tone of voice, sex, race, age, accent even, influence the answers given. As Hoinville and Jowell explain:

> 'Respondents may misunderstand a question, interviewers may make recording errors, answers may not be truthful: an obviously middle-class, middle-aged interviewer, for instance, may cause some respondents to express views they do not hold; a rather severe interviewer may intimidate a nervous respondent and cause him to give incorrect answers; the respondent may want to create a certain impression of himself to the interviewer; he may feel that certain answers are expected of him.'

> (Hoinville and Jowell 1978)

However the interviewer is only one of the participants in an interview situation albeit the dominant one. The respondent too can influence the discussion and even what is recorded. He/she is not the dumb, passive provider of information depicted in the textbooks; he/she too comes to the interview situation with certain aims, expectations, and a role to perform – what Agnew and Pyke (1969) have called 'On Stage Effect'. Respondents feel that they are on trial, they want to look their best, and so they may either give the answers they think the interviewer wants (or ought) to hear or alternatively be very guarded and evasive. Thus an interview situation, even when in an official place such as a police station or tax office, is a social encounter, a dynamic interaction in which the official seeks to extract 'objective' information and the respondent (for complicated and often unconscious reasons) frequently resists.

The second problem with interview data is that even if people are totally truthful, the 'abnormal' situation of the interview has only elicited what people 'say' they would do. You still do not necessarily know that this is how they will act in normal everyday situations – they may not even know that themselves. As Moss and Goldstein report (1979), the Central Office of Information found that surveys on the wearing of seat belts were always exaggerated and so it reverted simply to observing how many people actually used seat belts in real life.

Data analysis and interpretation

Ironically in comparison with studies on questionnaires and interviews there is a lack of studies in this area although it is just as important. Once interviews have been conducted the data collected has to be coded, usually for computer use, and the results analyzed. The same is true of official forms and although this may seem a purely mechanical and straight-forward task it has plenty of room for error; the more so the more 'open' the questionnaire, because more judgements about appropriate categories or codes will be necessary. All the clerk or data analyst has before him or her for judging what the respondent meant is what the interviewer has written. Thus errors may range from simply pressing the wrong key (and even the census has thousands of these to cope with (see p. 28) to making an error of judgement/inter-pretation as to the correct category for a particular response. There is also the danger highlighted by Julius Roth's revelations of coder laziness, confusion, dishonesty, and even cheating to get this often quite tedious task over and done with.

'The most expedient method of coding a few of the trickier open questions was to put down a "4" (this was the middle-of-the road response on the one question that had the most variation). If the responses were not clear or comprehensible, the coder had two alternatives: on the one hand he could puzzle over it and ask for other opinions or, on the other hand, he could assign it an arbitrary number, or forget the response entirely.'

(Roth 1966)

Finally the collated data has to be interpreted and presented. Not only is this a highly skilled job but one that raises major problems of validity. As you might expect with the official statistics on such topics as marriage and divorce, far from speaking for themselves the very same facts and figures will quite happily support totally opposite viewpoints. So it is always vital to examine how far the conclusions reached are actually supported by the data collected or whether there are elements of bias, exaggeration, and so on.

What is always very interesting about most official (and academic) publications is the very neat and highly structured way arguments and conclusions are presented. Rarely if ever are the problems and uncertainties about the reliability or validity of the data collected ever aired. Rarely do you get any insight at all into the many problems that must have existed in conducting a particular survey or study. There is no human drama; rather it is all presented as a highly professional, almost mechanical achievement, so that the reader will have no doubts about the reliability of the data and therefore few concerns or questions about the conclusions. The reality of data collection, as writers like Marten Shipman (1972) argue, is very different. Often research reports are 'packaged', the awkward bits left out, masses of statistics used (more as 'window dressing' than as collaborating evidence) and the intrusion of personal opinions and subjective values unconsciously covered up by 'impersonal' phrases or, worse, jargonese to make it appear truly 'scientific'. None of this 'behind the scenes' drama is ever allowed to cast a shadow over an official report, but there are now a number of sociological collections which do reveal the human face of academic research – and fascinating reading they make too if you enjoy 'Crossroads' or 'Dallas'. Studies like Jennifer Platt's (1976) and Bell and Newby (1977) reveal some of the personal struggles, frustrations, and even bitterness that lie behind some of the famous studies you may have heard of. What such revelations also highlight is the inevitable influence of personal views and values, not just on the interpretation of data but also on the way it was collected. As Marten Shipman points out:

> 'The natural science model assumes that the researcher eliminates his own influence as part of the total control over extraneous factors. But the impossibility of imposing technical controls when the researcher is part of the situation he is investigating is now well documented. The selection of topics, the design of research and the way results are analysed are always loaded with the assumptions of the researcher.'
>
> (Shipman 1976)

Ann Oakley's criticism (in Roberts 1981) of the textbook model of the research process goes even deeper. She sees its stress on 'objectivity' and rational judgement, its rejection of subjective feelings and emotions, as a very one-sided and artificial approach that reflects an underlying male bias. It cuts out or deprecates certain crucial influences on human behaviour and puts respondents generally – and women in particular – in an inferior position. Thus even this stage of the data-collecting process is fraught with the dangers of value judgements, ideological bias, personal feelings and ambitions – all the more so as such important influences are rarely acknowledged.

Sponsorship

This is in fact the first stage of the research process but also the last as it is the sponsor who will want to see and judge the final results. Though the term 'sponsor' is usually only used with reference to commercial organizations and market research, it is as relevant to ask why an official survey or registration was made, by which department and for what purposes, rather than merely accepting that because the government is sponsoring it there must be a good reason, an 'administrative' need. So much information is now collected on people by official (and unofficial) organizations that we have to have a Data Protection Act (1984) to ensure that it is accurate, confidential, and not misused. It is equally relevant to ask why certain social statistics are *not* collected, why certain groups (especially the rich and powerful) are able to evade official scrutiny in a way the rest of us are not. Like any other sponsor, government departments have a fairly clear idea of the answer they want to get and so attempt to influence the questionnaire and the final report; and if they are not happy with the results they will commission someone else. Royal commissions are a classic government method for collecting facts and figures on a major issue without necessarily having to do anything. As Harold Wilson once quipped, "they can take minutes and waste years" (quoted in Burton and Carlen 1979).

The theory of data collection

It is issues like these that show that far from being a straightforward technical procedure, the collection of official statistics is in fact a highly social, even political process. So much so that Nicholas Bateson, an ex-member of the coding department of the Social Surveys Division of the OPCS, has argued that surveys (and instruments like registers) are not merely means of data collection but also systems of data 'construction'.

'I use this term in preference to the conventional "data collection" or "data gathering" in order to stress that survey data are not, as their name would indicate,

126

"givens", waiting to be picked like flowers in a hedgerow. They are made, not found. ... The researcher selects a topic for investigation and then frames a question about this topic which gives structure or shape to the answer. In an interview survey additional shaping is given to the answer by the interviewer through the supplementary questions (or 'probes') that she improvises and the comments that she feeds back to the person she is interviewing and, when her work is finished and the questionnaire is returned to the researcher's office, coders and editors will continue to shape and to prune until the answer is reduced to a symbol standing for category membership – a code.'

(Bateson 1984)

It is through this process that knowledge is 'produced' and such a production process involves four key elements; the *client*, the *researcher*, the *informant*, and the *social world*. Therefore, unlike the natural scientist who can observe nature directly, the social researcher has to rely on second-hand information from the informant. He/she in turn is no expert and may have only passing acquaintance with the information required. Survey data is therefore 'third-hand knowledge' or worse, because the researcher and informant may not be in tune, may not be using the same 'language'; there is always plenty of room for misinterpretation and usually no effective way of checking the reliability of the data collected. It is all rather done on trust. The role of the researcher, therefore, is that of an *interpreter*. He has to *translate* the sponsor's aims into questions the informant can understand, and then *retranslate* his/her answers into a presentable and unified package acceptable to the sponsor, decorated with suitable statistics and correlations.

We have therefore three types of social knowledge, with the researcher trying to bridge the gap between his client's concepts and his informant's everyday knowledge:

(a) Knowledge as *information*, held in the heads of informants and organized in the natural language of everyday life;

(b) Knowledge as *data*, constructed by the researcher using the standard measurement operations of the survey method and organized in the form of a classification scheme;

(c) Knowledge as *expertise*, held in the head of the survey client and organized in the form of summary values on variables and relationships among variables.

The 'real' social world of the informant thus has to be recategorized into neat packages, into 'data matrices' to use the research jargon, and in so doing the opportunities for mistranslation, simplification, and even manipulation are obviously considerable. The key questions here are how accurately and validly do the final statistics relate to the real world as perceived by the informant (and we have already discussed possible reasons why informants may not give an accurate picture). Opinion data is especially unstable, especially open to being influenced – even created – by the measuring instrument, the survey. Thus for Bateson the crucial task for researchers, both official and academic, is to develop (in the absence of objective standards as in natural science) effective *validation* techniques: 'Survey data are valid to the extent that they meet the needs for knowledge of the survey client (and hence are relevant) and at the same time represent the social world (and hence are accurate).'

This is no easy task. All too easily the informant's views or perspectives on reality take second place to what the researcher thinks are his client's needs, so producing a false or invalid picture of social reality. Thus Bateson (1984) hopes to integrate the theory of social research with the practice – two elements all too often regarded as separate issues – and in so doing to show that far from statistics and other data speaking for themselves, they are constructed as the end product of a complex process of social interaction and knowledge production in which those who sponsor the research have a strong influence over the results produced.

The practice of official data collection

In one of the very few 'inside' accounts of how the GSS works, an anonymous group of official statisticians described the official data processing machinery in an article in *Demystifying Social Statistics* (Irvine, Miles, and Evans 1979). As a conclusion to this section it is worth reviewing it briefly as it sums up so many of the points above. As these officials explain, 'There is little awareness of the ways in which official statistics are produced' due to official secrecy and lack of interest, yet such an awareness 'is crucial to an understanding of the meaning of official statistics'.

As we saw in Part I, official statistics are produced primarily for administrative and political use. The needs of academics and businessmen come a poor second. Second, although the GSS is made up of a variety of semi-autonomous organizations it is essentially a government machine into whose values and ways of thinking even statisticians are carefully socialized, and in which tight control is maintained by strict rules, red tape, and the Official Secrets Act. As in all bureaucracies tight control from the top is maintained by the separation of thought and action. Whilst the ministers and mandarins formulate policy, the statisticians draw up the appropriate concepts, definitions, and categories. They design the official forms and the lowest clerical grades do the coding and card-punching. The results are analyzed and interpreted by the statisticians and passed back up the line to the administrators to develop and justify policies. It is this control from the top of the concepts and definitions themselves, of what is and is not to be collected, that really exemplifies the official control over knowledge:

'The methods and concepts developed and used for official statistics are shaped by the sorts of policies powerful people in the state wish to consider and by the concerns which preoccupy them. These concerns determine, at least partly, which phenomena are to be investigated as "social problems", and which neglected.'

(Irvine, Miles, and Evans 1979)

And once established, this hold over what knowledge is produced is virtually impossible to break.

This whole official data-collecting process centres around the official form or return sent out to various business organizations, local authorities, police stations, etc. Inevitably mistakes are made and though most are detected or at least escape the glare of publicity some do not.

'One example was when, following the accidental omission of a zero an Olivetti employee reporting the firm's exports, an under-estimate of national exports (and thus an over-estimate of the excess of imports over exports) generated a phoney balance of payments crisis. Another was when the trade figures went haywire over a period of many months because a clerk at one point copied two lines of figures on to a coding sheet in the wrong order.'

(Irvine, Miles, and Evans 1979)

And these are only the errors that are discovered. Most errors cannot be because there is no way of checking up whether businesses, schools, hospitals, and the like have provided accurate information when processing millions of forms a year:

'The data processing state is marked above all by tedium. The DHSS computer centre handles millions of medical certificates per year, the Inland Revenue centre millions of forms from tax offices. Storeroom attendants spend their days keeping track of the bundles of paper taken to and from the long dusty shelves. Clerks sit in rows in large open-plan rooms (designed so that everyone is visible to the supervisor) and sort out the forms into categories, or put every nth form aside for processing of a sample. Supervisors make spot checks and try to keep to schedule. All to the sound of soft piped pop music year after year.

The computer, supposed to usher in an age of automated freedom from clerical toil, has so far merely raised the productivity of boredom, and added new varieties of routine work to the old ones.'

(Irvine, Miles, and Evans 1979)

The clerical staff therefore have little interest and generally little knowledge of the data they are processing and the statisticians are under constant pressure for results, so inevitably the quality of the data suffers through inadequate analysis and over-simplification. Finally and only occasionally the statistics are manipulated. Outright fabrication is very rare:

'More common tactics include non-publication ("the truth, nothing but the truth, and as little of the truth as possible"), delay of publication, (such as the six-month delay of "race" statistics by Crossman, who feared the reaction to projections of the number of "immigrants"), misleading or inadequate commentaries on published figures (for example, being "optimistic" about the economic situation), and "massage".'

(Irvine, Miles, and Evans 1979)

Conclusions

This overview of the way official statistics are collected (or, as several writers have claimed, created) clearly questions the traditional idea that the social scientist or official merely digs up such facts and figures, slowly shuffling the pieces together until a clear picture of social reality emerges. Rather, beneath the packaged veneer, the statistical charts, and the scientific jargon lies a much more imprecise process which is on occasions subject to serious problems of both reliability and validity.

Second, it severely questions the claim by officials and social scientists that the whole process is entirely a technical matter in which neither they nor their subject-matter are influenced by outside factors nor by their own values and interests. Instead, as we have seen, the whole data-collection process is a highly social, even political activity in which human values and assumptions are an integral part of what data is collected and how it is interpreted.

Third, it seriously questions the 'scientific' assumption that social reality is essentially the same as the reality of the natural world – stable, fixed, and measurable – that social facts are the same as natural ones, and that social research techniques like the register or survey are therefore capable simply of collecting up the facts, measuring them, and deriving cause and effect relationships from them. As we have seen, an interview situation is more a dynamic and interpretative interrelationship than a simple 'fact-finding expedition'.

Further it ignores the importance of language, which not only acts as an avenue of communication between respondent and interpreter but is the medium through which we actually 'create' our concepts, definitions, categories, and relationships. As we saw throughout Part II, 'meaning' is crucial to social research and the meanings of social variables like poverty and crime are rarely fixed but are relative to particular situations. No social fact speaks for itself. It involves values and needs some sort of conceptual or theoretical framework to give it life and meaning, as this passage from C.W. Mills so clearly explains:

'The first rule for understanding the human condition is that men live in second-hand worlds; they are aware of much more than they have personally experienced; and their own experience is always indirect. No man stands alone confronting a world of solid facts. ... In their everyday lives the experience of men is itself selected by stereotyped meanings and shaped by ready made interpretations. Their images of the world . . . are given to them by crowds of witnesses they have never met and never will meet. Yet for every man these images – provided by strangers and dead men – are the very basis of his life as a human being. For most of what men call solid fact, sound interpretation, suitable presentation, every man is increasingly dependent on the observation posts, the interpretation centres, the presentation depots, which in contemporary society are established by means of what I am going to call the cultural apparatus.'

(C. Wright Mills, 'The Cultural Apparatus', a radio talk given on BBC Third Programme, March 1959)

Official statistics and social knowledge

The whole of our discussion so far, and particularly our discussion of how official statistics are collected and created, has clearly led us in to the depths and dangers of the sociology of knowledge. An examination of official statistics as the purest form of official knowledge provides excellent material for such key debates in sociology as those over the nature of social reality and the possibility of establishing objectivity and even truth. Unfortunately we do not have the space to follow the debate on official statistics to such an ultimate conclusion, though the whole topic of the sociology of knowledge is tackled in a companion volume in this series.

What is vital to note, though, is that although throughout this book we have severely questioned and criticized statistical data and official statistics in particular, this does *not* mean that such facts and figures are worthless or meaningless. Far from it. They are a vital and rich source of social information. They simply need handling with care. As even such radical writers as the authors of *Demystifying Social Statistics* (Irvine, Miles, and Evans 1979) argue, such an approach requires both a critical analysis of official statistics *and* the development of alternative sources of facts and figures. Examples of such 'unofficial statistics' include the various publications listed in Appendix A, such as the Low Pay Unit, Labour Research, and the Counter Information Services. By these means you will, I hope, learn how to handle all social statistics safely, and so learn what they really mean.

Finale

So at last you have arrived at the end of this statistical journey. You have travelled through many jungles of official statistics and even come face to face with some of the natives who live there. You have been given a statistical 'Green Cross Code' (pp. 14–15) and many lessons in the dangers that await those who venture into official statistics unarmed and unwarned. In particular you have been told always to look right to check their *reliability* and left to check their *validity*. Furthermore you have been taken below the surface to examine how such nuggets of knowledge are made and in whose image, to listen to different views as to what they mean and whom they represent and, most important, how they change shape, how a different picture of society unfolds depending on whose lens (or perspective) you use to examine them. They are a form of knowledge and so a form of power.

Now you are home and dry, you should check your equipment, go over what you have learnt, and practise it. Send for copies of official and unofficial statistics listed in Appendix A. Get used to backing up your arguments and your essays with appropriate facts and figures, dazzle your friends and teachers, but *always* add a note of caution, always check your sources, your footnotes, and who sponsored them. Develop a healthy scepticism, never take any statistics at face value, cross-check them against other sources (and against your own common-sense), and even when a detailed picture emerges think how different it would look from a Marxist, feminist, or phenomenological viewpoint. Look for the underlying theory, the taken-for-granted assumption, and then all other aspects of your sociological understanding will improve.

I hope you have enjoyed this statistical expedition and now feel confident and proficient enough to try some ventures of your own. Good luck!

Activities

1. Get hold of an official form from the post office or a government department and try to fill it in. Comment on how easy or difficult you found it, ways it could be improved and make a list of the possible facts and figures officials might have derived from it.
2. On p. 121 you were shown the enormous variety of ways even such simple words as 'children' and 'household' have been misinterpreted. Read the introduction to the 1981 census form (Appendix B) and questions H1, H3, and H5, and list possible misinterpretations.
3. What does Nicholas Bateson mean when he says survey data is 'third-hand knowledge?' (p. 127). What does C.W. Mills mean when he says we live in 'second-hand worlds'? (p. 132).

Further reading

There is very little directly on this issue though a lot on the problems of sociological research. Recommended 'inside' stories of research projects are the collections by Bell and Newby (1977) and Marten Shipman (1976) plus Shipman's 1972 critique. Derek Phillips' (1971 and 1973) view of sociological methods is always very thought-provoking.

Studies of social theory and knowledge tend to lose most students in the realms of abstract ideas and complicated concepts after page three. The various volumes by John Hughes for the Longman series are some of the most accessible (1980 and with Benson 1983 and Ackroyd 1981). Ian Cribb's attempt (1984) to bring social theory down to earth is quite readable and Glover and Strawbridge's small volume (1985) is quite good on the sociology of knowledge.

Recommended further reading

There are only a few studies of official statistics. For those willing to delve deeply the series by W. F. Maunders, *Reviews of UK Statistical Sources*, is worth dipping into! The best radical critique of official statistics is Irvine, Miles, and Evans (1979) *Demystifying Social Statistics*. The Open University series DE 304 and D 291 are both worth looking at for those who really want to learn more about this topic.

The 'Society Today' articles produced by *New Society* are always very useful as summaries. On the topics discussed in this book look at the following – they are written for 'O' and 'A' level students:

- 'Official Statistics' (18 November, 1982);
- 'Unemployment' (30 November, 1980);
- 'Marriage and Divorce' (13 and 20 November, 1980);
- 'Knowledge' (3 March, 1983);
- 'The Black Economy' (3 November, 1983);

- 'The Police' (10 May, 1984);
- 'The Future of Work' (8 and 15 November, 1985).

The *State of the Nation* by Fothergill and Vincent (1985) is a beautifully illustrated volume covering a whole range of social issues from a critical perspective. Its charts and graphs dramatically illustrate just how much about modern Britain can be pieced together from official statistics.

Appendix A
Official and unofficial
sources of statistics

Official statistics

The main official publications were outlined in Chapter 2.
Most of these are available in the reference section of public
or university libraries. Below, though, are some addresses of
government departments that may supply you with their own
up-to-date facts and figures:

1. The Central Statistical Office, Great George Street,
   London SW1P 3AQ.
2. The Ministry of Defence, Stats (G), 5 Northumberland
   House, London WC2N 5BP.
3. The Department of Education and Science, Elizabeth
   House, 39 York Road, London SE1 7PH.
4. The Department of Employment, Orphanage Road,
   Watford, Herts WD1 1PJ.
5. The Department of Energy, Thames House South,
   Millbank, London SW1P 4QJ.

6. The Department of the Environment, 2 Marsham Street, London SW1P 3EB.
7. The Department of Health and Social Security, Central Office, Newcastle-upon-Tyne NE98 1YX.
8. The Home Office, Tolworth Tower, Surbiton, Surrey KT6 7DS.
9. The Inland Revenue, Somerset House, The Strand, London WC2R 1LB.
10. Office of Population Censuses and Surveys, St Catherine's House, 10 Kingsway, London WC2B 6JP.
11. HM Treasury, Parliament Street, London SW1P 3AG.

Information and help is available from the Statistics and Market Intelligence Library, 1 Victoria Street, London SW1H OET, or the Information Services Division Room 58/G, Government Offices, Great George Street, London SW1P 3AQ, or the Business Statistics Office, Cardiff Road, Newport, Gwent NPT 1XG.

The OPCS has a lot of material specially prepared for schools, some free!

Unofficial statistics

1. Campaign for Press and Broadcasting Freedom/Counter-Information Services, c/o 9 Poland Street, London W1V 3DG.
2. Child Poverty Action Group, 1 Macklin Street, London WC2B 5NA.
3. Commission for Racial Equality, Information Department, Elliot House, 10–12 Allington Street, London SW1E 5EH.
4. The Conservative Party, 32 Smith Square, London SW1P 3HH.
5. The Employment Institute (Charter for Jobs) PO Box 474, London NW3 4SZ.
6. The Equal Opportunities Commission, Overseas House, Quay Street, Manchester M3 3HN.

7. The Labour Party, 150 Walworth Road, London SE17 1JT.
8. Labour Research Department, 78 Blackfriars Road, London SE1 8HF.
9. The Low Pay Unit, 9 Upper Berkeley Street, London W1H 8BY.
10. The National Council for Civil Liberties and Cobden Trust, 21 Tabard Street, London SE1 4LA.
11. The Policy Studies Institute, 100 Park Village East, London NW1 3SR.
12. The Race Relations Board, 5 Lower Belgrave Street, London SW1.
13. The Radical Statistics Group, c/o 9 Poland Street, London W1V 3DG.
14. Shelter, 157 Waterloo Street, London SE1 8XF.
15. The Unemployment Unit, c/o 9 Poland Street, London W1V 3DG.
16. The United Nations Information Service, 14/15 Stratford Place, London W1.
17. Women's Research and Resources Centre, 158 North Gower Street, London NW1.

Radical Statistics Group publications that are of special interest:

- *The Unofficial Guide to Official Statistics*;
- *Britain's Black Population*;
- *The Nuclear Numbers Game.*

Appendix B
The 1981 census form –
'edited highlights'

In the space available we can only reproduce page one of the 1981 census form. Nevertheless it tells you a lot about how official statistics are 'collected' and how the official mind works.

(The design of the census form is Crown copyright and is reproduced with the permission of the Controller of HMSO.)

In strict confidence

1981 Census England

H Form for Private Households

A household comprises either one person living alone or a group of persons (who may or may not be related) living at the same address with common housekeeping. Persons staying temporarily with the household are included.

To the Head or Joint Heads or members of the Household

Please complete this census form and have it ready to be collected by the census enumerator for your area. He or she will call for the form on **Monday 6 April 1981** or soon after. If you are not sure how to complete any of the entries on the form, the enumerator will be glad to help you when he calls. He will also need to check that you have filled in all the entries.

This census is being held in accordance with a decision made by Parliament. The leaflet headed 'Census 1981' describes why it is necessary and how the information will be used. Completion of this form is compulsory under the Census Act 1920. If you refuse to complete it, or if you give false information, you may have to pay a fine of up to £50.

Your replies will be treated in STRICT CONFIDENCE. They will be used to produce statistics but your name and address will NOT be fed into the census computer. After the census, the forms will be locked away for 100 years before they are passed to the Public Record Office.

If any member of the household who is age 16 or over does not wish you or other members of the household to see his or her personal information, then please ask the enumerator for an extra form and an envelope. The enumerator will then explain how to proceed.

When you have completed the form, please sign the declaration in Panel C on the last page.

A R THATCHER
Registrar General

Office of Population Censuses and Surveys
PO Box 200 Portsmouth PO2 8HH
Telephone 0329-42511

Please answer questions H1 - H5 about your household's accommodation, check the answers in Panel A, answer questions 1-16 overleaf and Panel B on the back page. Where boxes are provided please answer by putting a tick against the answer which applies. For example, if the answer to the marital status question is 'Single', tick box 1 thus:

1 ☑ Single

Please use ink or ballpoint pen.

To be completed by the Enumerator

Census District	Enumeration District	Form Number

Name ....

Address ....

....

.... Postcode

Panel A

To be completed by the Enumerator and amended, if necessary, by the person(s) signing this form.

This household's accommodation is:

- In a caravan ☐ 20
- In any other mobile or temporary structure ☐ 30
- In a purpose-built block of flats or maisonettes ☐ 12
- In any other permanent building in which the entrance from outside the building is

  NOT SHARED with another household ☐ 10

  SHARED with another household ☐ 11

H1 Rooms

Please count the rooms in your household's accommodation.

Do not count:

small kitchens, that is those under 2 metres (6ft 6ins) wide, bathrooms, WCs

Number of rooms ....

Note
Rooms divided by curtains or portable screens count as one, those divided by a fixed or sliding partition count as two.
Rooms used solely for business, professional or trade purposes should be excluded

H2 Tenure

How do you and your household occupy your accommodation? Please tick the appropriate box.

As an owner occupier (including purchase by mortgage):

1 ☐ of freehold property

2 ☐ of leasehold property

By renting, rent free or by lease:

3 ☐ from a local authority (council or New Town)

4 ☐ with a job, shop, farm or other business

5 ☐ from a housing association or charitable trust

6 ☐ furnished from a private landlord, company or other organisation

7 ☐ unfurnished from a private landlord, company or other organisation

In some other way:

☐ Please give details

Note
a If the accommodation is occupied by lease originally granted for, or since extended to, more than 21 years, tick box .
b If a share in the property is being bought under an arrangement with a local authority, New Town corporation or housing association (for example, shared ownership (equity sharing), a co ownership scheme) tick box 1 or 2 as appropriate.

H3 Amenities

Has your household use of the following amenities on these premises? Please tick the appropriate boxes.

- A fixed bath or shower permanently connected to a water supply and a waste pipe

1 ☐ YES - for use only by this household

2 ☐ YES - for use also by another household

3 ☐ NO fixed bath or shower

- A flush toilet (WC) with entrance inside the building

1 ☐ YES - for use only by this household

2 ☐ YES - for use also by another household

3 ☐ NO inside flush toilet (WC)

- A flush toilet (WC) with entrance outside the building

1 ☐ YES - for use only by this household

2 ☐ YES - for use also by another household

3 ☐ NO outside flush toilet (WC)

H4 Please answer this question if box 11 in Panel A is ticked

Are your rooms (not counting a bathroom or WC) enclosed behind your own front door inside the building?

1 ☐ YES   2 ☐ NO

If your household has only one room (not including a bathroom or WC) please answer 'YES'

H5 Cars and vans

Please tick the appropriate box to indicate the number of cars and vans normally available for use by you or members of your household (other than visitors).

0 ☐ None
1 ☐ One
2 ☐ Two
3 ☐ Three or more

Include any car or van provided by employers if normally available for use by you or members of your household but **exclude** vans used solely for the carriage of goods.

142

References

Ackroyd, S. and Hughes, J. (1981) *Data Collection in Context*. London: Longman.

Agnew, N. and Pyke, S. (1969) *The Science Game*. Englewood Cliffs, NJ: Prentice Hall.

Atkinson, A. B. (1972) *Unequal Shares; Wealth in Britain*. London: Allen Lane.

Atkinson, J. M. (1978) *Discovering Suicide*. London: Macmillan.

Atkinson, J. M., Kessel, and Dalgaard. (1975) The Comparability of Suicide Rates. *British Journal of Psychology* 21.

Bateson, N. (1984) *Data Construction in Social Surveys*. London: Allen and Unwin.

Bell, C. and Newby, H. (1977) *Doing Sociological Research*. London: Allen and Unwin.

Bellini, J. (1984) The Tax Avoidance Boom. *The Listener*, 5 April.

Belson, W. A. (1981) *The Design and Understanding of Survey Questions*. Aldershot: Gower.

Benson, D. and Hughes, J. (1983) *The Perspective of Ethnomethodology*. London: Longman.

Bottomley, K. and Coleman, C. (1981) *Understanding Crime Rates*. Aldershot: Gower.

143

Box, S. (1983) *Power, Crime and Mystification*. London: Tavistock.

Brand, J. (1975) The Politics of Social Indicators. *British Journal of Sociology* 26: 78–90.

Brenner, M. H. (1973) Mental Illness and the Economy. Unemployment, Economic Growth and Mortality. *Lancet* (Mar): 672.

Brynner, J. and Stribley, K. M. (eds) (1978) *Social Research Principles and Procedures*. London: Open University/Longman.

Bulmer, M. (ed.) (1978) *Social Policy Research*. London: Macmillan.

— (1980) 'Why Don't Sociologists Make More Use of Official Statistics?' *Sociology* 14: 505–25.

Burton, F. and Carlen, P. (1979) *Official Discourse*. London: Routledge & Kegan Paul.

Carley, M. (1981) *Social Measurement and Social Indicators*. London: Allen and Unwin.

Central Statistical Office (annual publication) *Economic Trends*. London: HMSO.

Child Poverty Action Group (1984) *Poverty: What Poverty?* London: CPAG.

Cicourel, A. (1976) *The Social Organisation of Juvenile Justice*. London: Heinemann.

Cohen, A. K. (1955) *Delinquent Boys*. Glencoe: Free Press.

Cohen, S. (1971) *Images of Deviance*. Harmondsworth: Penguin.

Cribb, I. (1984) *Modern Social Theory*. Brighton: Wheatsheaf.

Cripps, F. (1981) *Manifesto*. London: Pan.

Diamond Report (Royal Commission on the Distribution of Income and Wealth) (1975) *Initial Report on the Standing Reference* (report no. 1). Cmnd 6171. London: HMSO.

— (1976) *Second Report on the Standing Reference* (report no. 4). Cmnd 6626. London: HMSO.

— (1977) *Third Report on the Standing Reference* (report no. 5). Cmnd 6999. London: HMSO.

Donnison, D. (1982) *The Politics of Poverty*. Oxford: Martin Robertson.

Douglas, J. D. (1967) *The Social Meanings of Suicide*. Princeton: University Press.

Downes, D. and Rock, P. (1982) *Understanding Deviance*. Oxford: Oxford University Press.

Durkheim, E. (1970) *Suicide: A Study in Sociology*. London: Routledge & Kegan Paul.

Equal Opportunities Commission (1980) Research Bulletin No. 4, autumn 1980. Women and Government Statistics.

144

Eversley, D. and Köllman, W. (eds) (1982) *Population Change and Social Planning*. London: Edward Arnold.

Field, F. (ed.) (1979) *The Wealth Report I*. London: Routledge & Kegan Paul.

— (ed.) (1983) *The Wealth Report II*. London: Routledge & Kegan Paul.

Fothergill, S. and Vincent, J. (1985) *The State of the Nation*. London: Pluto.

Glover, D. and Strawbridge, S. (1985) *The Sociology of Knowledge*. Ormskirk: Causeway.

Glyn, A. (1984) The Economic Case against Pit Closures. Pamphlet from the NUM, St James House, Vicar Lane, Sheffield, South Yorkshire S1 2EX.

Goldthorpe, J. and Lockwood, D. (1968) *The Affluent Worker*. Cambridge: Cambridge University Press.

Gomm, R. and McNeill, P. (eds) (1982) *A Handbook for Sociology Teachers*. London: Heinemann.

Government Statistical Service (annual publication since 1970) *Social Trends*. London: HMSO.

Hakim, C. (1982) *Secondary Analysis in Social Research*. London: Allen and Unwin.

Halsey, A. H. (1978) Class Ridden Prosperity. *The Listener*, (19 January).

Handy, C. (1984) *The Future of Work*. Oxford: Blackwell.

Harbury, C. and Hitchens, D. (1977) Wealth, Women and Inheritance. *Economic Journal*. March.

— (1980) The Myth of the Self-made Man. *New Statesman*. 15 February.

Hastings, W. M. (1979) *How to Think about Social Problems*. New York: Oxford University Press.

Higgins, J. (1985) *Poverty: Developments in Sociology*, edited by M. Haralambos. Ormskirk: Causeway.

Hird, L. and Irvine, J. (1979) The Poverty of Wealth Statistics. In J. Irvine, I. Miles, and J. Evans (eds) *Demystifying Social Statistics*. London: Pluto.

Hite, S. (1977) *The Hite Report*. New York: Wildwood House.

Hoinville, G. and Jowell, R. (1978) *Survey Research Practice*. London: Heinemann.

Home Office Research Study (No. 76) (1983) *The British Crime Survey*.

Hooke, R. (1983) *How to Tell the Liars from the Statisticians*. New

145

York: Marcel Dekker.

Hubback, D. (1983) *Population Trends in Great Britain: Their Policy Implications*. London: Policy Studies Institute.

Huff, D. (1973) *How to Lie with Statistics*. Harmondsworth: Penguin.

Hughes, J. (1980) *The Philosophy of Social Research*. London: Longman.

Institute of Fiscal Studies (1985) quoted in the *Guardian*, 18 July.

Irvine, J., Miles, I., and Evans, J. (1979) *Demystifying Social Statistics*. London: Pluto.

Jowell, R. and Airey, C. (1984) *British Social Attitudes*. Aldershot: Gower.

Kahn, R. L. and Cannell, C. F. (1963) *The Dynamics of Interviewing*. New York: John Wiley.

Kinsey, A.C., Wardell, B., and Pomeroy, C. E. M. (1948) *Sexual Behaviour in the Human Male*. Philadelphia: Saunders.

— (1953) *Sexual Behaviour in the Human Female*. Philadelphia: Saunders.

Labour Research Dept (1985) *Breaking the Nation*. London: Pluto.

Leonard, E. (1982) *Women, Crime and Society*. New York: Longman.

Maunders, W. F. (1974 onwards) *Reviews of UK Statistical Sources*. London: Heinemann.

McCarthy, P. D. and Walsh, D. (1966) Suicide in Dublin. *British Medical Journal*, 1: 1393–396.

McNeill, P. (1985) *Research Methods*. London: Tavistock.

Merrit, G. (1982) *World Out of Work*. London: Collins.

Merton, R.K. (1968) *Social Theory and Social Structure*. New York: Free Press.

Miles, I. (1975) Numerical Moralities. Paper to the 1975 Radical Statistics Conference.

Miller, W. B. (1962) Lower Class Culture as a Generating Milieu of Gang Delinquency. In M. E. Wolfgang, L. Savitz, and N. Johnston (eds) *The Sociology of Crime and Delinquency*. New York: Wiley.

Moss, L. and Goldstein, H. (eds) (1979) *The Recall Method in Social Surveys*. Windsor: NFER.

Muncie, J. (1984) *The Trouble with Kids Today*. London: Hutchinson.

Newman, D. (1956) Pleading Guilty for Considerations. *Journal of*

Criminology, Law and Police Science 46, 6 (March–April): 780–90.

Orwell, G. (1937). *The Road to Wigan Pier*. London: Gollancz.

Osman, T. (1985) *The Facts of Everyday Life*. London: Faber and Faber.

Parkin, F. (1972) *Class Inequality and Political Order*. St Albans: Paladin.

Phillips, D.L. (1971) *Knowledge from What?* Chicago: Rand McNally.

— (1973) *Abandoning Method*. San Francisco: Jossey-Bass.

Pickett, K. (1974) *Sources of Official Data*. London: Longman.

Platt, J. (1976) *The Realities of Social Research*. London: Sussex University Press.

Presidential Commission (1967) *Report on Law Enforcement and Administration of Justice*. Washington DC: US Government Printing Office.

Radzinowicz, L. and King, J. (1979) *The Growth of Crime*. Harmondsworth: Penguin.

Reichmann, W. J. (1964) *The Use and Abuse of Statistics*. Harmondsworth: Penguin.

Reid, I. (1981) *Social Class Differences in Britain*. London: Grant McIntyre.

Reid, I. and Wormald, E. (1982) *Sex Differences in Britain*. London: Grant McIntyre.

Rhind, D. (ed.) (1983) *A Census User's Handbook*. London: Methuen.

Roberts, H. (ed.) (1981) *Doing Feminist Research*. London: Routledge & Kegan Paul.

Roberts, K. (1983) *Youth and Leisure*. London: Allen & Unwin.

Roberts, K , Cook, F. G., Clark, S. C., and Semeonoff, E. (1977) *The Fragmentary Class Structure*. London: Heinemann.

Roth, J. (1966) Hired Hand Research. *American Sociologist* 1: 190–96.

Rutter, M. and Giller, H. (1983) *Juvenile Delinquency, Trends and Perspectives*. Harmondsworth: Penguin.

Sanders, D. (1976) *Statistics: A Fresh Approach*. New York: McGraw Hill.

Seabrook, J. (1982) *Unemployment*. St Albans: Paladin/Granada.

Shipman, M. (1972) *The Limitations of Social Research*. London: Longman.

Shipman, M. (ed.) (1976) *The Organisation and Impact of Social Research*. London: Routledge & Kegan Paul.

Sinfield, A. and Fraser, N. (1985) *The Real Cost of Unemployment*. Edinburgh: Department of Social Administration, University of Edinburgh.

Smith, D. J. (1983) *Police and People in London*. London: Policy Studies Institute.

Smith, D. J. and Gray, J. (1983) *Police and People in London*. London: Policy Studies Institute.

Stengel, E. (1964) *Suicide and Attempted Suicide*. Harmondsworth: Penguin.

Taylor, I., Walton, P., and Young, J. (1975) *The New Criminology*. London: Routledge & Kegan Paul.

Thatcher, A. R. (1984) A Review of the 1981 Census on Population in England and Wales. *Population Trends* 36, summer: 5–9.

Thomas, D. (1985) Taking the Measure of Unemployment. *New Society*, 16 May.

Townsend, P. (1979) *Poverty in the United Kingdom*. Harmondsworth: Penguin.

— (1984) *Why the Many Poor?* Fabian pamphlet no. 500.

Townsend, P. and Davidson, N. (1980) *Inequalities in Health*. Harmondsworth: Penguin.

UN Multilingual Demographic Dictionary (1958) quoted in G. D. Mitchell (1979) *A New Dictionary of Sociology* London: Routledge & Kegan Paul.

Walker, R., Lawson, R., and Townsend, P. (eds) (1984) *Responses to Poverty: Lessons from Europe*. London: Heinemann.

Williams, M. (1985) *Britain Now Quiz*. London: Longman.

Index